"Much has been written about brain-based learning recently, but most fall short when looking for a comprehensive treatment of the topic. In *Education for the Human Brain: A Road Map to Natural Learning in Schools*, Timothy B. Jones provides a complete treatment of the subject. I would recommend it to anyone who is looking for an up-to-date and innovative book on natural and brain-compatible learning." —**Fred C. Lunenburg**, PhD, Jimmy N. Merchant Professor of Education, Sam Houston State University, Texas

"This definitive work about the brain, learning, and education will help school leaders plot a course for their instructional leadership thinking. In doing that, it reveals questions that must be dealt with in making 'ethical decisions'—providing the answers that leaders must evaluate in making instructional choices. Too often in the past leaders have been handed prescriptions for educating our young citizens—decisions made by the uninformed and those whose values are all about money, control, and expedience. This volume helps one cut through the noise and debris in making meaningful educational and instructional decisions." —**James A. Vornberg**, Regents Professor, Texas A&M University-Commerce

"In *Education for the Human Brain*, Timothy B. Jones and his colleagues offer insights into a most powerful tool for transforming instruction and learning—the brain. Dr. Jones assembled this group to chronicle their joint experiences in training and modeling practices for school leaders who choose to accept the challenge of changing school operation and leading improved learning for all children. I will use this book in my instructional theory class." —**George W. Moore**, PhD, associate professor, Sam Houston State University

"*Education for the Human Brain: A Road Map for Natural Learning in Schools* is timely and greatly needed as education continues to be a hot public issue. Dr. Jones and his cadre of industry experts have operationalized the complex task of changing how learning occurs using a process that almost any educational leader can follow. The 'road map' facilitates implementation of the latest innovations in instruction by utilizing the professional learning community to make a difference for all learners! Bravo!"—**Russell W. Marshall**, EdD, superintendent, Mabank Independent School District

Education for the Human Brain

A Road Map to Natural Learning in Schools

Edited by
Timothy B. Jones

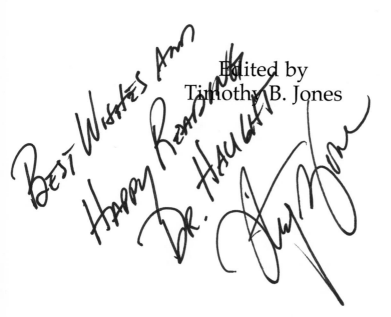

ROWMAN & LITTLEFIELD EDUCATION

A division of
ROWMAN & LITTLEFIELD PUBLISHERS, INC.
Lanham • New York • Toronto • Plymouth, UK

Published by Rowman & Littlefield Education
A division of Rowman & Littlefield Publishers, Inc.
A wholly owned subsidary of The Rowman & Littlefield Publishing Group, Inc.
4501 Forbes Boulevard, Suite 200, Lanham, Maryland 20706
www.rowman.com

10 Thornbury Road, Plymouth PL6 7PP, United Kingdom

British Library Cataloguing in Publication Information Available

Library of Congress Cataloging-in-Publication Data

Education for the human brain : a roadmap to natural learning in schools /
edited by Timothy B. Jones.
    pages cm
  ISBN 978-1-4758-0092-0 (cloth : alk. paper) — ISBN 978-1-4758-0093-7
(pbk. : alk. paper) — ISBN 978-1-4758-0094-4 (ebook) 1. Learning,
Psychology of. 2. Cognition in children. I. Jones, Timothy B.
  LB1060.E35 2013
  370.15'23—dc23

                                                            2013007400

∞™ The paper used in this publication meets the minimum requirements of
American National Standard for Information Sciences—Permanence of
Paper for Printed Library Materials, ANSI/NISO Z39.48-1992.

Printed in the United States of America

The book is lovingly dedicated to my mother and brother.

Gladys Marie Hemphill Jones has been not only the world's best mom but also always my biggest fan. I know I got from her my love of reading, which certainly parlayed into my love of learning, but I have the warmest memories of her reading to me classics I would have never read on my own. She taught me that working hard means being passionate and committed and that being short is a good thing and nothing to hold me (or her) back. But most importantly she continues to inspire me to dream, and that coupled with her unconditional love is the greatest gift she could give me.

My brother, Jeffrey Allen Jones, MD, and I get closer as we get older, as I am sure most siblings do. As I worked on this book and looked back on the work that preceded its writing, I am struck at how much *courage for risk taking* I learned from him. He taught me this through his own life—a life that often travels the road never taken or even the road that does not exist. As he navigated his life, he gave me the courage and maybe even some permission to navigate mine similarly. Although I know at times our willingness and enthusiasm for changing course or taking new chances has been stressful or even difficult for our family, I also know that it was those events, those changes, and specifically those risks that have given both of us incredibly rich and fulfilling careers and lives.

and to every professional educator who has dreamed and taken a chance for the betterment of the children in our care each day . . . bravo!

Contents

Foreword

Anyone writing a book about the brain and education for practitioners has to walk a fine line. On the one hand, it needs to be true to research, and the unfortunate truth is that the researchers do not always agree with each other. On the other hand, it must be useful to those in the trenches, and they (quite legitimately) have neither the time nor the interest in plowing through the arcane language and vast mass of detail that accompanies most research.

But even the very notion of putting research into practice poses a problem. Educators today are caught between several rocks and hard places. There is a sense of urgency and a need to improve performance *now*. It seems as though the only acceptable indicator of success is improved test scores, when the evidence is quite clear that simply aiming to raise test scores is not the way to go. Then there are those who say, "Tell me what I can do on Monday," as though brain-based learning is reducible to a set of simple strategies that can be demonstrated and implemented immediately. That is not correct.

One of the reasons that I so like this book is that Timothy B. Jones and his colleagues have managed to walk much of that fine line. In so doing, they have demonstrated a fine understanding of the complexity of teaching and school turnaround. I would like to clarify the point by identifying some of the factors that are crucial to success and that are either articulated by the authors or are implicit in their actions.

IT'S NOT JUST THE BRAIN

The word "brain" was emphasized in the early years of brain-based learning because it was felt that the emerging field of neuroscience added both information and credibility to the processes that were being implemented. But it is always about brain and mind. There always needs to be a blend of research from neuroscience and psychology and education. Some of that is apparent in this book.

IT'S NOT JUST A COLLECTION OF STRATEGIES

Success depends upon grasping an underlying philosophy, a way of framing everything so that sometimes strategies are acquired but sometimes they can simply be invented. The process is about helping students understand more deeply. It is inherently constructivist (even though there can be a great deal of direct instruction). And this book spells out that constructivist philosophy.

IT'S NEVER JUST ABOUT TEACHING

Every aspect of schooling is connected to every other aspect. If, for instance, the goal is to create a safe environment in which students can take risks, it also needs to be safe for the teachers and administrators to take risks. And because educators develop at different rates, the entire ambience of a school and the ways in which people communicate are critical, as is the general approach to standards, testing, involvement of the local community, and so on. This book helps to reveal that the issue involves system-wide change and a more sophisticated way of thinking about systems.

SUCCESSFUL CHANGE TAKES TIME

All the chapters on practice demonstrate quite clearly an appreciation of the fact that the process cannot be hurried. There will always be bumps in the road and the challenge and tension of changing the ways that we think about the fundamentals of our profession. *Education for the Human Brain* helps to give readers room to breathe, and that is one of the greatest gifts possible for any educator at any time.

GREAT LEADERSHIP IS VITAL

I have been invited on countless occasions to talk about or introduce brain-based learning by administrators who know little and care less. Successful change cannot proceed from that foundation. Leaders must be present. They must commit adequate resources. They must participate— even if they are also learning at the same time. And this book is a testament to great leaders and an awareness of the demands of great leadership.

It has been a pleasure working with Dr. Jones since the days of his first Summer Principal's Institute in 2001. It is extremely refreshing to be part of a gathering of authors that blends theory and practice so equitably. And I am very happy to commend a book that calls for hard work but with an approach that makes it highly probable that the hard work will pay off. Congratulations to all.

Geoffrey Caine
www.CaineLearning.com
Idyllwild, California

Acknowledgments

This book is the culmination of almost twenty years of work. Consequently, it is a labor of love involving many people over that entire period. At the risk of leaving someone out, I want to acknowledge these important people without whom this book would not have been possible.

First, I want to thank Tom Koerner, vice president and editorial director at Rowman & Littlefield. As a new author navigating new territory, I could not have received more encouragement and help from Tom. Tom believed in my vision for this work from the very beginning, and it was comforting knowing he was there to guide and assist me at each turn in the process.

My quantum leap into brain research and learning started during my administrative career in the Nacogdoches Independent School District and conception of the Silver Team. Starting a program that abandons traditional instruction takes courage, and I am not just talking about my own! For James G. Partin, superintendent of schools, Sandra Sherman, assistant superintendent of curriculum and instruction, and especially Steve Green, principal of Thomas J. Rusk (TJR) Middle School, I thank you for the great courage you had in letting me build the academic program of my dreams and then supporting me, the teachers, and the students in every way possible. Each of you epitomizes risk taking and moral leadership, and I am grateful to have had the opportunity to work with each of you.

When I started the Silver Team at TJR, I asked the teachers I interviewed if they could let go of every inclination (or behavior) they had about learning and traditional classes. Sharon Hill and Michelle Hooper exponentially stepped up, and the three of us reinvented learning and the learning environment for forty-two eighth-grade students in our first year and eighty-four seventh- and eighth-grade students in each year thereafter. Like the other administrators listed above, Sharon and Michelle were amazingly courageous in finding a better way for children to learn. These are two of the finest educators I have known in my career, and I am grateful for all they taught me and the friendship that culminated. The impact of this program on our students and their families coupled with the attention it brought to our district still to this day astounds me.

Speaking of that attention, most educational leaders work their entire career without most people, certainly outside of the school, knowing about much of their work. As a young administrator, imagine my surprise when I was contacted by KLRN-TV, the PBS affiliate in San Antonio, asking to include us in a Texas Education Agency project called Promising Practices in Texas Education. C. A. Messina and Mary Leahy, producers, brought such value to our program in the way they told our story primarily through the words of our students and teachers. I am grateful to both of them for seeing what we had to offer and why it was important to tell others. This publicity brought many visitors to our school, which certainly inspired me to want to further operationalize (i.e., become a student of learning and learning environments) the success we were having so that I might share it with others. The buzz they created continues today, and I continue to be grateful.

One such avenue for helping schools become brain-compatible was with my dear friend Ross B. Sherman, who cofounded with me the Principal and Superintendent Institute at the University of Texas at Tyler. The institute provided funds for developing materials and seminars to help school leaders and teachers transform learning in their schools. Drs. Russell Marshall and Peggy B. Gill joined our efforts as permanent faculty members, as did Geoffrey Caine, whose book *Education on the Edge of Possibility*, written with his wife, Renate, inspired each of us and guided our years of work with schools. Geoffrey not only worked with each member of the institute every year but also became a great friend and inspiration to me. To each of the institute staff, thank you for the hard work, the years of experience you shared, and for the useful insights and processes that have become this book.

Every successful person has mentors, and one of the most valuable to me has been first, my major adviser in my doctoral program at Stephen F. Austin State University, and now my esteemed colleague and friend

Patrick M. Jenlink. Dr. Jenlink introduced me to John Dewey and constructivism, which forever changed my vision about schools and learning. Without Dr. Jenlink's introduction, the body of work we present herein would simply have not been possible; his inspiration has ultimately impacted thousands of students in the schools in which I have had the opportunity to work since the Silver Team.

To my colleagues and the staff in the Department of Educational Leadership and Counseling at Sam Houston State University, I give kudos and deep thanks. Sam Houston State is a wonderful and supportive place for an academic to work. I am particularly thankful to Stacey Edmonson, Julie Combs, George Moore, John R. Slate, Tony Onwuegbuzie, and Debbie Allen for their many deeds and constant support of me and my intellectual endeavors. I could not ask for better colleagues.

I also thank Dr. David Barrett, one of my former doctoral students who provided counsel and editing assistance as the draft of this book became final. Dave's intellect and sense of humor made him an incredible student in my class but now an even better colleague and friend. The final manuscript was better because of his insights and numerous contributions. I look forward to many more collaborative projects with him in the future.

To all of the schools and school districts I have worked with over the years, I give thanks! You have allowed us on your campuses and in your classrooms. Thank you for the opportunity to work with you, your staff, and your students. More importantly, thank you for all that you taught us along the way. We hope this book will help share your success and lessons with other educators.

And finally, to each of the contributors of this book I offer my thanks, admiration, and sincere esteem and devotion. I have worked with each of them, many of whom have been individually mentioned earlier, on my brain/mind learning journey over the past fifteen-plus years. Absent any one of these authors-leaders and the record that is this book would be incomplete. I cannot imagine another educator that has been able to work with a more competent, insightful, and inspirational group of colleagues than I have with this group. For you, thank you for your contributions to this book, but more importantly, thank you for being part of me both professionally and personally.

Thank you all for substantially helping me create and now pen my own professional quilt. My immense gratitude to each of you!

Introduction

Education for the Human Brain: A Road Map to Natural Learning in Schools

Timothy B. Jones

Hierarchy and behaviorism: What do these words evoke for you? Do they evoke images of twenty-first-century learning, or do they provide flashbacks to a different age? For more than 150 years, public schools have largely been hierarchal organizational structures that were operationally grounded in behavioral teaching theory. More recently, postmodern thinking has yielded the "learning community" as an organizational strategy to replace or at least augment the hierarchal structure while still maintaining the behavioral teaching approaches. Consequently, how learning looks in the classroom has remained largely unchanged.

Over the past three decades and perhaps even longer, most everyone with any interest in public education has weighed in on the discussions of school reform, restructuring, redesigning, or change in schools in general. The motives for such dialogue are as varied as the dialogue itself. Should the public education system fix what it has, start over from scratch, or simply abandon the system all together? All of these options have certainly been considered. Is the problem with educators themselves? Is our public system too expensive and inefficient? Should we give parents the opportunity to take public money and use it for private education?

Scholars, experts, commissions, think tanks, politicians, state and federal agencies, teachers, administrators, and community members have all had something to say on the subject in one way or another. Pressures to better the system from these stakeholders have resulted in higher accountability, more student testing, new alternatives in education, and worse, perhaps, more skepticism of the public school system itself. Hundreds if not thousands of books and articles have been written, and millions if not billions of dollars have been spent, yet most would agree that little has substantively changed in the average public school classroom. The twenty-first-century school is merely a row or collection of one-room schoolhouses conveniently joined together under one roof yet maintaining the ideals, mission, models, and methods of the agrarian time period in which it was created.

Like so many paradoxes in public educational leadership, the purpose of this book shares commonalities with other works, and yet it is also different. Like others written, we will chronicle what we know about schools and learning and how our work has made them better; we will make a compelling argument for the need to rethink how learning occurs in the classroom in light of what we know about how the brain learns; we will provide a process and vehicle for school leaders and other stakeholders to chart a path of continuous betterment of schools; and we will offer new ideas and technologies to assist with the new paradigm of school dynamics. Our effort will embrace six important premises:

1. Public schools are a cornerstone of American democracy and the American dream. Public schools are a critical component of the American economy and provide the best choice for a quality education. The American public will be best served by investing in the restructuring of public schools instead of the creation of alternative educational options.
2. Making schools better for all learners does not mean fixing what we have; rather, it means reconceptualizing what we do in schools and how we do it. Schools and school leaders need to reexamine age-old issues, structures, models, and instructional and curricular challenges with a different perceptual orientation and frame of reference.
3. Schools that will be significantly better will be not only different from what is regarded as the traditional school but also wholly unique; there is no panacea or cookie cutter for great schools other than strong leaders and a focused purpose. These schools will be different: organizationally poised to learn and grow, particularly pedagogically because of advances in brain research, human potential, computer technologies, and a revitalized focus on constant and continuous betterment.
4. School improvement and success is measured not by performance on standardized minimum-skills tests but rather in overtly striving to meet the individual potential of learners.

5. Professional educators have an ethical obligation to document and share their experiences, knowledge, and innovations with the educational profession and academia.
6. The principal is not the only key leader in making schools better. In fact, a number of different school leaders can fundamentally change learning and help teachers transform learning in their classrooms using the latest practices and pedagogy.

So what makes *Education for the Human Brain* unique? In addition to being a book on the cutting edge of best practice and pedagogy, we have successfully done everything we prescribe for you, our reader. This book is a chronicle or reflection of the schools we have started; schools we have helped; leaders we have taught, coached, and advised; and programs we have impacted with results that we publish. Each contributor to this book has worked with me directly in one or more of the events of my practice, including starting my own school within a school; developing processes to help others do the same; establishing an institute of experts for collaborating with and teaching school leaders and schools; and consulting with leaders to help advance learning outcomes on their campuses or in their school districts.

Among us we have more than two hundred years of experience in education, and our work reaches two dozen states and several countries and has impacted thousands and thousands of students. This book is our attempt to cohesively provide our collective experience and expertise to anyone interested in schools and making every classroom an environment for fostering each student's individual potential. Our approach begins by replacing the strict hierarchal structure in schools and school districts with the Professional Learning Communities. Moreover, our approach also replaces the behavioral teaching theory that is intrinsically teacher centered (and thus counterproductive to being learner centered) with a constructivist approach that is brain compatible. Our book also presents two case studies of real-life, successful implementation by different levels of administrative leadership and at differing levels of learners. These case studies were written by the leaders themselves, and they tell their story in their own voice so as to coach the reader. Anecdotes of many other leaders that have taken this approach are also offered in different parts of the book.

Kurt Vonnegut, the American writer, said that to open a book "is to arrive in a music hall and be handed a viola. You have to perform." In order to facilitate your performance in this educational concerto, this book has been divided into three parts: "Exploration," "Inspiration," and "The Road Map."

EXPLORATION:
UNDERSTANDING THE BRAIN AND LEARNING

First, we believe there is a heightened sense of urgency for schools to not only be better but also be better competitors in a growing industry. This part of the book is designed to equip you with valuable information for navigating the waters and politics of the school enterprise, including assessment and testing. Next, this section will explore the science of natural and brain-compatible learning and end with a detailed discussion on the learning theory (as opposed to teaching theory) known as constructivism and how it supports natural learning and brain compatibility.

INSPIRATION: CASE STUDIES OF SUCCESS

In part II, two cases studies are presented to illustrate to you the success of our approach to learning and schools. The case-study chapters are written by the leaders involved in these initiatives and chronicle their journey of school change and natural learning. Included in these case studies are the good, the bad, and the ugly to inspire and inform you in your practice. Each study will conclude with performance data from state-mandated assessments as everything in the book is offered within the context of the reality of high-stakes testing. The stories told present two approaches with a very different look and feel of brain-compatible learning but are clearly similarly grounded in a learner-focused environment and approach. This highlights the adaptability of this approach. It is not a one-size-fits-all model.

THE ROAD MAP: PLANNING
AND IMPLEMENTING THE WORK AHEAD

Finally, our road map of implementing natural and brain-compatible learning at any level and in any content area is presented and discussed.

We believe that there is no cookie cutter for a great school or school program. Instead, we believe that great learning comes from a variety of different school leaders, and our road map is designed to help anyone in that capacity. We believe that the Professional Learning Community provides a fluid and dynamic structure for a school organization that constantly learns and betters itself. Our "cogito" process for creating innovative schools is a simple and ongoing approach for building and facilitating a school culture conducive to best practice and learner focus. It further provides a structure for sustaining itself and growing as human resources change and improve.

Finally, this section will seek to motivate you as you contemplate the massive task of school change, and you will hear from people that have taken this plunge and the results of their hard work. We hope you will get a sense of hope and courage as you dream of better student learning for your school or schools regardless of your formal role within the school. We have worked with principals, assistants, teachers, curriculum directors, counselors, superintendents, and everyone in between. Ultimately, it is about what goes on in each individual classroom, and there are lots of ways leaders impact those classrooms.

School leadership is about calculated and informed risks necessary to systemically better student learning on an ongoing basis. The thirteen contributors of this book have spent a career dreaming about better schools and taking the risks necessary to bring those schools into reality by embracing a fundamentally different perspective of the traditional school and classroom. These authors bring an extensive cadre of experiences to the quality education discussion in our roles as teachers, building and central office administrators, college professors, community members, and parents.

For our courageous colleagues (anyone reading this book), we reflect and share in what follows our best efforts and knowledge of student learning, achievement, and performance. We commend your desire to make learning better, and we hope this will help you dream and take the risks necessary to do it! Together, we can make beautiful music for our learners!

Part I

EXPLORATION

Understanding the Brain and Learning

The first part of the book is designed to explore brain research and natural learning and the issues in education that surround it. Because accountability is such a critical part of schools, this exploration is done within that context.

The first chapter will explore the current conditions in public education and make an argument for making substantial changes to the method in which children learn. Chapter 2 will contextualize education within the current accountability lens and discuss how the brain should function in that context. In chapter 3, the science and principles of how we learn naturally will be explored as well as what that means for the brain and schools. Finally, chapter 4 will explore constructivism as an instructional method and philosophy for educators to facilitate a transformation to brain-compatible and natural learning in schools.

Upon concluding part I, "Exploration," the following critical beliefs and paradigms will begin to emerge:

- We believe that educators have not kept sufficiently current on emerging trends and research-based practices in quality instruction and therefore are not on the cutting edge of essential, relevant technologies and strategies.
- We believe that advances in the neurosciences have not resulted in widespread application of current teaching practices in the United States and have denied learners a better opportunity for long-term memory penetration resulting in better student performance.
- We believe that public schools must acknowledge that to compete and regain market share from other educational alternatives, educators must

become more responsive to our consumer through comprehensive, continuous improvement.

- We believe that increased accountability is not only good for education but also necessary for creating and maintaining excellence for all learners, but such accountability cannot be focused on minimal skills.
- We believe that traditional instruction continues to mainly focus on the behavior of the teacher instead of the learning of the student and is not natural for the human brain. The constructivist classroom is process driven and intrinsically motivational by placing responsibility and ownership of learning on the student, resulting in the authentic, relevant construction of knowledge.

Chapter One

The Why!

Timothy B. Jones

We argue that ultimately the key to really effective education is to align the best of what is known about learning and teaching with systems that facilitate such learning and teaching, appropriately supported by the larger culture within which education occurs. The alignment may, but will not necessarily, occur in the United States. However, there is absolutely no doubt that those communities that grasp and implement such an alignment will develop a vastly superior system of education, and in the medium to long term they will clearly have a significant competitive edge.

—Geoffrey Caine and Renate Caine (2001)

Neuroscience, and what has been learned about the human brain and how it processes and learns, is arguably the biggest breakthrough in education in more than a hundred years. Yet, as the quote above suggests, the United States may be lagging behind many other countries that have navigated a route for implementing its incredible technologies. For some time in the United States, public education has been under fire for lackluster student performance, some of which is warranted and some of which is not. Worse, it is professional educators, instead of the system, who are now being targeted as the problem by politicians and some political think tanks.

Perhaps any discussion on school change or systemic improvement efforts should start with the question of why. Why change our 150-plus-year-old model of public education that, by some account, has been successful in creating an educated electorate as necessary for our democracy? Is it simply a political issue of the day, or is it time for fundamental change in order to improve education in a complex and ever-changing economy? Certainly, if we are to make a compelling argument for school leaders to take on the enormous task of substantial school change, then the question of why bother in the first place needs to be addressed. In this chapter, our argument for developing more innovative and pedagogically advanced schools will be presented as well as a discussion on what has prevented it to date. Not only will this information be critical for understanding the immediate need to navigate instructional change in many schools, but also the information will assist any school leader who desires to develop and implement natural learning on their campus through brain-compatible pedagogy in building the support and infrastructure necessary for successful implementation. This is tough work, and information is key to embarking on this journey.

WHY CHANGE LEARNING IN SCHOOLS?

Although we believe there are dozens of reasons to fundamentally change instruction and innovation in schools, we will concentrate our argument on four primary areas of concern: competition, advances in the neurosciences, accountability, and an outdated mental model and theoretical grounding. We have selected these areas because they address not only why school leaders need to take action but also why they need to take action now. The urgency we believe exists for public school change is paramount.

Competition

In the fall of 2013, arguably the highest percentage of school-age children in the history of the U.S. educational system chose an alternative for their education from the traditional public school. This is a trend that has continued for the past two dozen or so years. An expansion of school choice, private schools, charter schools, and home schools, to name a few, continue to increase their market share of school-age children. For example, home-schooling research has suggested that by 2025 as many as one in four school-age children may be home schooled. Charter schools are opening all across the nation at a staggering pace. Private schools are benefiting from huge endowments and often offer the same benefits of public schools yet have students and parents who perceive the value to be higher than the public school counterparts.

In the business world, this phenomenon would be regarded as competition. As educators, we do not like to think of ourselves as being in business or that we compete for customers, but the reality is that we are and we do. If our public school consumer was satisfied with what we had to offer, then obviously there would be little or no need for the alternatives those consumers are choosing.

Moreover, the reality of this decline in public school market share has enormous implications. In business, a continuing decline in market share ultimately leads to the inability of the organization to sustain itself. Take General Motors as a perfect example. For many years, although profitable, General Motors continued to lose market share as their business model failed to compete in a changing market. Twenty years ago, no one would have predicted bankruptcy for the once largest corporation in the world, yet in 2009 they filed bankruptcy, which led to fundamental change to that business model, including substantial downsizing.

Seemingly, if the decline of market share continues for public schools, its viability also becomes in jeopardy. What is more disturbing is that despite the continuing loss of market share, educators and educational leaders do not seem to understand that not addressing the trend is actually contributing to the further decline in market share and thus contributing to the demise of public schools. Since the publishing of *A Nation at Risk* in the 1980s, billions of dollars have been spent on school reform, restructuring, and improvement efforts, yet very little has actually changed. The biggest change has been that more children have left the public school for some other educational alternative.

Additionally, political forces now want to add school vouchers in the name of further school choice. With a voucher program, parents in theory could put their child in any school they wish and the vast sums of money, both state funds and local property tax money, would follow the child in whatever option was selected. In theory, parents could use state money to place their child in the most prestigious private school in the community. We call it the Everyone Can Go to Harvard Theory. Of course, that isn't possible and would result in many students (mostly intellectually and economically advantaged) leaving the public school system on a quest for something more prestigious or better perceived while stripping critical resources from the public school system. School vouchers are a recipe for crippling the public school system by redistributing public money into other educational alternatives that provide little evidence (other than perception) of their effectiveness in educating all students or providing the best environments for learning.

Does that mean we believe public schools are going to die? To be sure, they most likely will not die during the careers of the contributors of this book. But should that be the objective? As professional educators and school leaders, can we simply continue to watch the decline in public schools' capacity to compete and still be good stewards of our profession and of our schools? The legacy of every professional educator should be his or her contribution to the continuation and improvement of public schools, not a contribution to its demise.

In short, our consumers, the people who fund our schools, increasingly believe public schools are not the best option for an education. Educators have traditionally pointed the finger at others for our plight, but as stewards of our profession, it is our responsibility, in fact our obligation, to lead the public school into centers of excellence for all learners. Every year we fail to do that, and thus continue to lose market share, we diminish our capacity to reverse the trend. To be clear, not only do we believe in public schools and a public education for all children, but also we believe it still offers the best choice for parents wanting to give their child a leg up on the world that awaits them.

Advances in the Neurosciences

It should not be a surprise that in the information age we know more about the brain today than we did forty years ago (Caine & Caine, 1994, 1997, 2001, 2008 [with McClintic & Klimek], 2011; Hardiman, 2012; Sousa, 2011). What is surprising is that what we now know has not systemically informed our pedagogical and curricular practice as educators. Educators in general do not understand how the brain learns, remembers, and retrieves information. While the concept of brain research and natural learning is becoming more common among staff development and in-service topics, the application of the concept has informed educational practice at an alarmingly slow pace.

Consider for a moment that many of the basic foundations of the traditional math curriculum (integers, operations, decimals, and fractions) are taught in multiple grades sometimes six or seven years in a row. If students learn and authentically apply the concepts the first time they are learned, then why do we need to reteach them year after year? The same can be said about many of the foundations of the language arts curriculum (parts of speech, sentence structure, and types of writing). These are just two small examples of curricular repetition that seemingly make learning inefficient.

Brain and mind research would suggest that this reality is a result of learning that is not transcending into the long-term or permanent memory of learners (Caine & Caine, 1994, 2011; Hardiman, 2012; Jensen, 1998; Sousa, 2011). In other words, if the learning finds its way into a learner's long-term memory, then the learning becomes permanent. Obviously, if students learn how to add fractions and that learning becomes part of his or her long-term memory, then the students do not need to learn it again and can instead expand and reinforce the learning in new constructed meaning.

How can public school educators defend this practice? Is it in the best interest of public schools and the professional educator profession to defend the current method when there is extensive evidence (much of which is our own observation with our students) that much of the learning does not remain with the learner? The advances in the neurosciences provide invaluable insights on learning and memory. Schools that do not embrace brain-based learning principles are indirectly attempting to defend our instructional practices and methods that do not result in authentic long-term learning.

In short, brain research has demonstrated that many common practices in public schools actually decrease brain activity in learners. Why would a professional teacher engage in a classroom activity that science knows decreases brain activity in the learner? There seems to be two reasons for this reality. First, research clearly documents that teachers teach the way they were taught, not necessarily the way they were taught to teach. Further, many teachers were prepared to teach using methods and strategies that were not yet informed by the advances in the neurosciences over the past two decades and therefore were not part of their teacher preparation program.

We believe that most teachers want to do what is best for students. Many of those teachers simply do what they know how to do, and to lead them to a new paradigm in instructional strategies will require quality professional development that is sustained and supported. Some teachers have these skills and use them; others have these skills and choose not to use them for some reason or another. Students learn best and efficiently when they learn naturally (Caine & Caine, 2011).

Second, teachers generally do what they perceive their principal expects them to do. If the principal expects learning to be passive and quiet, then the teacher delivers a classroom where learning is passive and quiet. If the principal believes that good teachers "stand and deliver," then the teachers stand and deliver. In contrast, if the principal expects learning to be active and exciting, then the teacher delivers a classroom that concentrates on students learning instead of teachers teaching. This type of learning looks different than traditional learning and may not seem like the controlled and quiet environment that many teachers believe their principals expect.

In sum, education that reflects the advances in neurosciences (and thus is on the cutting edge of the times) is education that is brain compatible and learning that is natural. Schools that are competitive will seek and understand the advances in the neurosciences so that learning is efficient and effective. The science of the brain and natural learning will receive greater focus in chapter 3. Similarly, chapter 4 will explore constructivism and how the construction of knowledge can serve as a learning model for natural learning in a brain-compatible school.

Accountability

Standards and expectations of public schools continue to rise. There is no evidence that this reality will not continue into the future. In fact, with the passage of No Child Left Behind (2002), there is compelling national evidence that standards and accountability of educators will continue to increase for the foreseeable future. The public wants more from the schools it funds, and they want the education profession to be accountable for what they do and how they do it.

Many professional educators have reacted negatively, often hostilely, about the accountability movement. The reality is that public education was largely unaccountable for more than a hundred years. This has arguably resulted in the educational profession becoming complacent. Some satisfaction studies have suggested that schools have not kept up with the times, and certainly the increased competition discussed earlier in this chapter supports that suggestion. The lack of accountability has contributed to the deteriorating confidence in the system by a variety of stakeholders. In contrast, the high-stakes testing that has accompanied accountability has refocused educators on minimum skill performance and not toward individual learner potential. Accountability presents another paradox, which has contributed to the lack of confidence in public schools.

The leaders of innovative schools centered on excellence understand that, without accountability, education will be complacent and unresponsive to its consumers. Professional educators that focus on excellence for all students do so by embracing and supporting a variety of performance measures and authentic assessments. Schools can focus on the individual potential of all learners while still being held accountable on minimum-skills standardized tests. Chapter 2 will further discuss the connections between the brain and accountability and how the brain-compatible classroom thrives in an environment of high-stakes testing.

An Outdated Model

When advocates for school change begin discussing a change in perceptual orientation, it is easy to conclude that the thought is abstract or too foreign to comprehend, much less actually apply. The truth is, however, the perceptual orientation of most educators is grounded in theory that is no longer regarded in scientific circles as valid. The fundamental theory that informs much of the work we do is no longer appropriately grounded. This is not to suggest that the theory is wrong or bad but rather to suggest that it was useful in a former time and that such grounding now prevents taking public education to a new level of excellence. It is a theory that was as revolutionary in its time as the line of thinking that is offered in its place is now. Consider the following:

> With the emergence of the atomic age, scientists since the early twentieth century were forced to call into question the very basic understanding that dated back to Descartes and Newton. This Cartesian and Newtonian thinking, overwhelmingly mechanistic and linear, was highly limited in grappling with and understanding atomic energy and theory, which was far more dynamic. It was these limitations that gave scientists an opportunity to

construct new forms, language and concepts that began to account for that
phenomenon. (Jones, 2013, p. 807)

The mental model that is woven into so much of the agrarian school
is theoretically grounded in the mechanistic and scientific model that developed into a modernist lens at the hand of Descartes and Newton. The
absolute nature of science and hence the scientific method as we know it
is grounded in the Cartesian assumption that nature's laws are a derivative
of mathematics and can be solely explained and accounted for in numbers.
This was Descartes's idea of certainty. Newton, contributing his now famous formula on gravity, influenced the modernist's orientation with his
vision of a symmetrical and stable universe of simple organization.

One such Cartesian principle that is prevalent in public schools is one
of his four methodological rules for seeking truth and understanding. The
rule in sum directed to divide things into as many parts as possible in
order to more easily understand them (Descartes, 1950). In fact, the idea
was to be applied to all matter. Logically, Descartes concluded, all matter
can be subdivided, and through the understanding of its parts we gain an
understanding of the whole. Alas, this theory provides the grounding for
our modernist perspective on curriculum: Break it up, explain the parts,
and at some point understand the whole. This thought, coupled with Newton's vision of a stable and geometrical universe of simple organization,
offers a specific orientation of science being absolute, of the scientific
method accounting for all phenomenon, and hence of the way we believed
the learning of truth occurred. The mechanistic thinking that so influenced
the Cartesian and Newtonian vision does not, however, provide for the
chaotic or complex order of the universe because such chaos or complexity cannot be explained mathematically.

So what is wrong with a modernist lens that has served us well for centu-
ries? Put simply, the theory, although useful in its time, is no longer valid.
The truth is that our world surrounds us with disequilibrium, chaos, and
turbulence. Quantum theory would suggest that living things in a complex
adaptive system only reach a state of equilibrium when they die (Wheatley,
2006). With the advances in quantum theory and atomic science, we have
proven the difficulty in subdividing matter. The atom, once believed to be
the smallest form of matter, when subdivided does not separate into parts,
and the atom was never the smallest part (Capra, 1997).

Even more interesting, most of an atom consists of vast amounts of space. The movement of the protons and neutrons are not predictable and instead yield nothing more than patterns of probability, but they are still in the context of its biggest component of vast sums of space that adapts as it connects and interacts with its surroundings or environment. We cannot conclude as they move from one place to another what path they travel or whether they actually travel at all. Simply stated, quantum physics calls into question all of our assumptions about the exact nature of science and the simple organization of the universe. Scientists have long since accepted the vast limitations of the Cartesian and Newtonian vision. Unfortunately, educators have not yet accepted those limitations, although they have attempted to use it in forming Professional Learning Communities (PLCs), which Peter Senge (2012) and Richard DuFour and colleagues (2010) clearly connect to this phenomenon, yet the process has not yielded any significant variation to Descartes's notion of matter as it pertains to curriculum.

Postmodernist perceptual orientation has evolved from a mechanistic vision to a vision that all living things are part of a complex, adaptive system. Hence, we have a new perceptual orientation known in science as systems thinking and complexity theory, which we can connect to brain-compatible and natural learning (Jones, 2013). It is this orientation that gave birth to the concept of the PLC. Imagine what schools and learning might look like if only they were not grounded in the concept that all matter can be subdivided. These new sciences have enormous implications on education, just as they have already had on science, economics, and business.

Any system change in paradigm, toward a postmodernist lens, will have to embattle our modernist, mechanistic vision if we are to be successful in changing instruction in schools. Innovative schools are built and sustained through learning communities (Caine & Caine, 2010; DuFour, DuFour, Eaker, & Many, 2010; Senge, 2012). Developing and utilizing a PLC as a process for fundamental school change will be further characterized in chapter 7.

OBSTACLES TO INNOVATION

There are clearly a multitude of reasons that schools have not changed toward brain-compatible and natural learning. Geoffrey Caine and

Renate Caine (1997, 1999 [with Crowell], 2001, 2008 [with McClintic & Klimek]) suggest that the educational profession has created a system that actually resists and prevents fundamental change in school culture and instructional practice. Most reasons for not engaging such change can be classified in one of three areas: (1) complexity of the task, (2) ineffective professional development, and (3) emphasizing product over process. Although we discuss each of these three areas separately, they are also tightly interconnected.

Complexity of the Task

In the last section, we characterized schools as being outdated and poorly grounded. Andy Hargreaves and Michael Fullan (1998) suggest that this outdated and inflexible system makes schooling "agonizingly difficult." John Brown and Cerylle Moffett (1999, p. vii) add that "these attempts at educational reform will not succeed without fundamental and heroic changes in the culture, structure, policies and perceptions of the place we call school." Caine and Caine (2001, 2010, 2011) document that this reality continues today.

True change, according to Senge (1999), occurs in an organization that is continually expanding its capacity to create its future. The principal then must institutionalize learning into its social fabric by defining and building an infrastructure that fosters and supports learning (Hutchens, 1998). Principals can cultivate learning communities in their schools when they lead with intentionality and heart (Uchiyama & Wolf, 2002).

It does not take much thought to realize that the type of cultural and instructional change we believe is critical for natural learning for children not only is complex but also will be arduous and time consuming. Caine and Caine (1997) argue, "This new paradigm will require a new type of person. The key to the emergence of that person—the possible human—is to better understand what human potential means in terms of brain research and other developments, and then to teach to actualize that potential" (p. ix). Changing people, much less than changing the lens in which they see, requires overt, systemic, continuous, and careful planning and empowerment. Such structures and systems are neither common in many public schools nor familiar to many school leaders. However, school administrators and teachers who have successfully implemented brain-compatible and natural learning in their schools and classrooms provide thoughts, observations, and anecdotal insights in chapter 10.

The innovative change of schools in the scope we suggest requires a well-informed school leader followed by a comprehensive and ongoing planning structure that will serve as a road map for facilitating and cultivating the PLC. Successful planning identifies a core ideology and a shared vision so that everyone in the PLC has a clear and definitive understanding of the mission and values of the school. The plan must allow for all members of the PLC to learn and transcend as part of the process through a targeted and comprehensive professional development. The plan is a living plan that constantly reassesses itself using student performance indicators and outcomes while involving the community in the ongoing improvement process. Chapter 8 will offer our schematic for developing and implementing such a comprehensive plan—a plan that has worked for many schools that have taken this step for learners in their school.

The complexity of the task can be conquered with strong leadership and a process and plan for facilitating the school toward continuous improvement. With such a complex task at hand, it is easy to see how educators can become apathetic or discouraged and their leaders conflicted. Such conflict can lead to fear. Dealing with the complexity of the task also means dealing with fear, apathy, and discouragement. Chapter 9 is designed to inspire the leader to have the courage to lead this difficult task despite these barriers. Involving and empowering the discouraged, the apathetic, and the fearful (including the leaders) is necessary and vital to the innovative change process.

Ineffective Professional Development

Research on high-performing schools point in one direction, starting with strong administrative leadership present in the organization. However, despite millions of dollars spent on school reform and improvement efforts, very little has systemically changed (Caine & Caine, 1994, 1997, 2001, 2008 [with McClintic & Klimek]).

A successful professional development program in schools must begin with a successful professional development program for principals. Roland Barth (2001) says that professional development for principals has

been described as a "wasteland." In-service education for school principals is often viewed by principals as something "done to" them by others
(Stevens, 2001). Moreover, the professional development principals are
offered is "impractical and focuses on the wrong things" (Johnson, 2002).
Common practices in staff development for principals are programs that
are topic specific, content loaded, short term, held out of district, and
appropriate for awareness-level conceptual development but not for the
ongoing nature necessary to build skills that lead to substantial behavior
change (Caldwell, 2001). Many attend, few succumb, and fewer learn
(Barth, 2001). The same argument can be made with many professional
development programs for teachers and other education personnel.

In order for schools to become cutting edge and innovative, principals
and teachers must engage in their own continuous improvement. Professional development must be tightly aligned with the ideology and beliefs
of the school and driven by the mission of the school. Most staff development models have proven to be ineffective in facilitating systemic change.
Chapter 8 will also outline a comprehensive program of professional development and discuss how to use the professional development program
as a vehicle for continuous improvement of teachers, yourself, and other
educational personnel.

Emphases on Product Instead of Process

John Dewey (1910) characterizes the ideal mental condition as being a
balance between work and play, drudgery and foolishness, and product
versus process. He reminds us that this sentiment was simply captured in
the old adage "all work and no play makes Jack a dull boy." As stated earlier, high-stakes testing and other accountability pressures have resulted in
schools focusing on minimum-skills performance instead of concentrating
on individual learning potential. Learning is highly individual. The idea
of learner-centeredness builds upon this idea. Learner-centered instruction is instruction that is designed to meet the individual learning needs
of all children. All children do not learn at the same pace, with the same
methods, or at the same time. They construct meaning and knowledge in
the context of their prior knowledge and their own individual experiences.

Instruction that is learner centered should enlighten and challenge
learners wherever they may be in the content of the curriculum. Learning should be and can be intrinsically motivational. But as Dewey (1910)

suggests, to achieve the ideal mental condition, learning must find a balance between the process of learning and the product of learning. Put differently, there should be as much value in the process of learning as there is in the product of learning. High-stakes testing places emphasis exclusively on the product of learning with little or no regard for the many lessons learned in the process of learning. When educators focus so much time on the standardized tests or meeting minimum skill objectives, learning becomes unmotivating and inefficient and forgoes the learner's natural opportunity for individual human potential. In sum, learning becomes unnatural! Even worse, when we concentrate exclusively on meeting minimal skills, many learners succumb to lower-level learning or learning that has already occurred.

Constructed meaning and knowledge is retained (Brooks & Brooks, 2001; Marlowe & Page, 2005). For learners to construct knowledge and meaning, they must be empowered to take responsibility and ownership for their learning and thus be active, not passive, in the learning process. In order for learners take an active role in their own learning, the process must have as much reward as does the product. Despite using terms such as "learner centered," traditional schooling remains incredibly behavioral, teacher centered, and teacher directed. Until teachers stop seeing their role in the learning process as the gatekeepers of the content, of the learning, education will continue to be teacher centered.

Students have the capacity to frame their own questions, direct their own inquiry, and predict their own theories as they learn the content associated with the standards in which we are held accountable. The process of learning should provide more lessons than just a minimal skills test at the end. This is achieved with learners guiding their own learning and by learning from each other. Constructivist learners own their learning and are therefore intrinsically motivated to continuously engage the process. Maria Montessori was one of the early practitioners of constructivism and the construction of knowledge. Chapter 5 presents a case study of how an early childhood school successfully implemented brain-compatible and natural learning using the Montessori model. As we strive to understand the PLC, we embrace that learning is natural, and the novelty of learning is its best reward.

The constructivist classroom aligns with the new paradigm of the new sciences and is grounded in cognitive science theory and brain-based learning. The constructivist classroom is not about giving and receiving, which is teacher centered, but rather it is about thinking and understanding, which is learner centered (Marlowe & Page, 2005). It is not about studying the parts of a television but rather about understanding how the parts work together and integrate with other systems. The constructivist classroom is learner centered and process rich. Constructivist learners think at high cognitive levels and process information at a higher level of complexity. The characteristics and benefits of the constructivist classroom will be outlined in chapter 4.

As we move away from simple, minimal skills standards and expectations for performance and toward higher expectations of all learners, we cannot continue to use the old methods of evaluation and assessment. While we will continue to be held accountable for minimum skills as measured by standardized testing, we must create new, richer forms of authentic assessment that supports the rewards of the process of learning as well as documents the product of learning. For example, in chapter 6, a director of mathematics in a large urban district chronicles her journey in transforming algebra classes from traditional sit-and-get instruction to brain-compatible learning that centered on critical thinking and problem solving. Likewise, chapter 2 will also provide an understanding of how brain-compatible learning will affect performance measures and what opportunities will be created for richer forms of evaluation and assessment.

CONCLUSION

In this chapter we have outlined our argument for implementing a brain-compatible and natural learning culture to improve schools and briefly discussed why we think it has not occurred already. Within this context, we outlined how this book can help school leaders overcome any detractors in order to systematically plan and implement an innovative instructional approach to learning in schools, so that student learning will become efficient and natural, and realize individual student potential.

REFERENCES

Barth, R. (2001). Principal centered professional development. *Theory into Practice, 25*(3), 156–160.

Brooks, J., & Brooks, M. (2001). *In search for understanding the case for constructivist classrooms.* Alexandria, VA: Association for Supervision and Curriculum Development.

Brown, J., & Moffett, C. (1999). *The hero's journey: How educators can transform schools and improve learning.* Alexandria, VA: Association for Supervision and Curriculum Development.

Caine, G., & Caine, R. N. (2010). *Strengthening and enriching your professional learning community: The art of learning together.* Alexandria, VA: Association for Supervision and Curriculum Development.

Caine, G., & Caine, R. N. (2001). *The brain, education, and the competitive edge.* Lanham, MD: Scarecrow.

Caine, G., & Caine, R. N. (1997). *Education on the edge of possibility.* Alexandria, VA: Association for Supervision and Curriculum Development.

Caine, G., Caine, R. N., & Crowell, S. (1999). *Mindshifts: A brain compatible process for professional development and the renewal of education.* Tucson, AZ: Zephyr Press.

Caine, R. N., & Caine, G. (2011). *Natural learning for a connected world: Education, technology, and the human brain.* New York: Teachers College Press.

Caine, R. N., & Caine, G. (1994). *Making connections: Teaching and the human brain.* Menlo Park, CA: Addison-Wesley.

Caine, R. N., Caine, G., McClintic, C. L., & Klimek, K. J. (2008). *Twelve brain/mind learning principles in action* (2nd ed.). London: Sage.

Caldwell, S. (2001). Effective practices for principals' in-service. *Theory into Practice, 25*(3), 174–178.

Capra, F. (1997). *The web of life: A scientific understanding of living systems.* New York: Anchor Books.

Descartes, R. (1950). *Discourse on method.* New York: Liberal Arts (Original French publication, 1637).

Dewey, J. (1910). *How we think.* New York: Prometheus Books.

Doll, W. (1993). *A post-modern perspective on curriculum.* New York: Teachers College Press.

DuFour, R., DuFour, R., Eaker, R., & Many, T. (2010). *Learning by doing: A handbook for professional learning communities at work.* Bloomington, IN: Solution-Tree.

Hardiman, M. (2012). *The brain-targeted teaching model for 21st century schools.* Thousand Oaks, CA: Corwin.

Hargreaves, A., & Fullan, M. (1998). *What's worth fighting for out there?* New York: Teachers College Press.

Hutchens, D. (1998). *Outlearning the wolves: Surviving and thriving in a learning organization.* Waltham, MA: Pegasus Communications.

Jenson, E. (1998). *Teaching with the brain in mind*. Alexandria, VA: Association for Supervision and Curriculum Development.

Johnson, J. (2002). Staying ahead of the game. *Educational Leadership, 59*(8), 26–32.

Jones, T. B. (2013). Complexity theory. In G. Brown, B. Irby, & R. Lara-Alecio (Eds.), *Handbook of educational theories*. Charlotte, NC: Information Age Publishing.

Jones, T. B. (2012). How exciting are schools for adults? *Insight: Journal of the Texas Association of School Administrators, 27*(4).

Jones, T. B. (2011). Schools find brain research key to student engagement and improving performance in math. *Insight: Journal of the Texas Association of School Administrators, 26*(3), 17–18.

Marlowe, B., & Page, M. (2005). *Creating and sustaining the constructivist classroom*. Thousand Oaks, CA: Corwin.

Senge, P. (Ed.). (2012). *Schools that learn*. New York: Doubleday.

Senge, P. (2006). *The fifth discipline: The art and practice of the learning organization*. New York: Doubleday.

Senge, P. (1999). *The dance of change: The challenges of sustaining momentum in learning organizations*. New York: Doubleday.

Short, P., & Greer, J. (2002). *Leadership in empowered schools: Themes from innovative efforts*. Upper Saddle River, NJ: Merrill Prentice Hall.

Sousa, D. A. (2011). *How the brain learns* (4th ed.). Thousand Oaks, CA: Corwin.

Stevens, K. (2001). Collaborative action research: An effective strategy for principal in-service. *Theory into Practice, 25*(3), 203–206.

Uchiyama, D. P., & Wolf, S. A. (2002). The best way to lead them. *Educational Leadership, 59*(8), 80.

Wheatley, M. (2006). *Leadership and the new science: Learning about organizations from an orderly universe*. San Francisco: Berrett-Koehler.

Wheatley, M. (2002). *Turning to one another: Simple conversation to restore hope to the future*. San Francisco: Berrett-Koehler.

Chapter Two

The Brain and High-Stakes Accountability Testing

Genie Bingham Linn

A true story . . .

It was the weekend after most schools had let out for the summer. Memorial Day shoppers fished through the sale racks at the department store. You can run but you can't hide when you spend your workdays presenting professional development sessions for ninety-eight school districts! I smiled when I recognized a face from a recent workshop, even though I didn't remember her name. Unwittingly, I gave the innocuous greeting "How are you?" I was unprepared for the response. Tears filled her eyes, "I don't know what to do." She fumbled to open her purse and showed me an envelope. "It's my letter of resignation. I don't know what to do with it. No one is on campus this week since school ended."

Stunned into an uncomfortable silence, I simply nodded and listened. "This has been such a hard year. Everyone on campus worked so hard to get our students ready for the test. We did everything we knew to do because another year of poor performance would be bad news for all of us. No matter what we did, the test results were not good. Yesterday as we left campus for the summer, the principal's parting words were, 'Next year the scores better go up or else!'" She took a deep, ragged breath, "I just can't take it anymore." Shaking her head to ward off tears, she apologized, "I'm sorry . . . I guess I will just mail this letter."

I can't remember what I said or did, but I can't forget how I felt. I felt angry and defeated along with her. What was to be done? I confess that when I was teaching ninth-grade English, I once gave in to the fear also. Despite what I knew and believed about teaching language arts, I joined my colleagues in numbing my students with reams of practice activities. I cratered to my fears. I lost my bravado and teaching confidence when I was the only one *not* using the test prep packages. I wish

I could apologize to those adolescents for the weeks of my panic and
our frustration.

Similar scenes are replayed over and over in schools across the nation. "I
used to teach math, but now I just teach the test." Look in any classroom
door in most schools and you are likely to see students working on test
preparation. Ask children what they are doing in January, and they will
likely tell you they are taking practice tests. Even though a significant
premise of brain-compatible learning is a safe environment, risk and
threat are typical elements in the everyday life for educators, students,
and parents in public schools. This reign of terror is the result of high-
stakes testing gone wild with high-stakes accountability in schools. Every
educator understands the value of assessment in instruction. Assessment
informs instruction. Good assessments are indicators of content and skills
mastered while giving educators directions for the next instructional steps
based on the indicated student needs.

Assessment is good and necessary, as is accountability. Since schools
have been entrusted with the care of children, a community's most valuable possessions, they should be accountable and responsible. In addition,
since schools are stewards of designated local, state, and federal funds,
they should also have an accounting for the use of these funds according
to the assigned purpose. Money marked for lunches, special education,
and other designated programs must be used in accordance with the
funding guidelines. Accounting for the use of the funds is expected, but
accountability and funding standards now demand results in student performance to align with spending. Schools must spend appropriately, and
in addition the spending must produce the desired performance results.
Consequently, assessment scores on high-stakes testing are the standard
measure for school accountability. Logically and reasonably leaders agree
that just as accountability is the standard for integrity in business practice,
so should it be the rule for education.

Businesses, banks, and government are guarded by the accounting rules
regarding money. Where did it come from? Where did it go? Money is
readily tracked, quantified, and accounted. Bank examiners comb through
records and data to verify accounting accuracy and lawful handling of
funds. The numbers are predictable, reliable, and constant according to
the accounting principles. The accounting results can be balanced and
rectified. Deposits and withdrawals, and profits and deficits, can be seen,

held, touched, and printed. Banks understand funding accountability, and they are answerable or liable for results.

Businesses conduct inventories of goods and services. Inputs and outputs are concrete evidence for which management is accountable. Businesses understand resource accountability. Government agencies accept the accounting principles and responsible spending by publishing budgets, tax revenues, and agency outlays. Line items govern the spending amount and purposes. Since government agencies are stewards of public funds, they are held accountable for spending appropriately and providing designated services.

Accounting and accountability have long been associated with the reasonable predictability of quantifiable figures. Accounting is the system of recording and summarizing business and financial transactions in books and analyzing, verifying, and reporting the results. Accounting and accountability are derived from reasonable mathematical and systemic concepts that can be controlled and predicted. Accountability has now become synonymous with education as "a policy of holding school and teachers accountable (responsible) for students' academic progress by linking such progress with funding for salaries, maintenance, materials and programs, etc." (Dictionary.com, n.d., paragraph 2). Educators are held responsible based on the often unpredictable and unreliable one-day performance of children on a high-stakes test. In effect, educators must place their professional lives in the hands of children.

Children who enter into public schools come in every size, shape, color, and ability level. They come from every ethnic group and socioeconomic background. They come from families that are equally diverse. Rich, poor, and in between, some have every advantage and some have every disadvantage. Children from disadvantaged homes are predictably the most at-risk learners. Public schools do not get to pick the "good" ones. They have no control of the "raw materials" that come into the school system, but they are all still accountable to produce the same high-quality student achievement. As one conference speaker said, "The best and quickest way to get higher test scores is to get better students!"

As a nation we have taken the two valuable and necessary practices—assessment and accountability—and created a system driven by high-stakes accountability testing that terrorizes educators, students, and communities. This has created an environment that is anathema to brain-enriched learning as educational stakeholders, students, parents, teachers, administrators, and school communities are running scared.

Despite the serious issues that have evolved in the wake of high-stakes accountability, this study does not intend to argue for or against. The purpose of this chapter is to encourage leaders to promote brain-compatible learning within the environment of high-stakes accountability testing. To begin this examination, the chapter provides a historical perspective of school accountability and the high-stakes assessments with the guiding question "How did we get here?" Further background in the chapter presents a look at the current results of the high-stakes environment by asking, "What is happening?" Finally, the study looks at the importance of a natural and brain-enriched learning environment using the guiding question "Where are we going?" Hopefully, addressing these questions will encourage leaders by providing them with information and understanding as they endeavor to nurture brain-enriched learning in a hostile environment of high-stakes accountability testing.

HOW DID WE GET HERE?

Without question, the authority behind high-stakes testing and accountability has come from the powerful federal mandates in No Child Left Behind (NCLB). NCLB was first authorized in 2001 under the administration of George W. Bush. Central to the administration of this authority is the assessment of student progress according to a system of state-designed standardized tests at significant educational points. These mandated assessments and measurement standards are enforced with sanctions and penalties for those who fail to meet the assigned performance levels for Adequate Yearly Progress (AYP). Since the enactment of NCLB, schools have felt the ominous shadow of AYP that follows with every test administration. The noble intent of NCLB, to ensure educational equity and equality for all children, has become lost in the darkness of penalty and punishments for low-performing schools. The unintended consequences have overwhelmed the intent. The Department of Education and the legislature are now challenged to reform the reform.

Before No Child Left Behind

Early in the nineteenth century, district school boards were elected and charged with ensuring that schools achieved the community goals. Yearly elections served as the accountability check. As school districts became larger, boards adopted standardized, short-answer high school entrance exams to assess progress toward achieving the district goals (Cuban, 2004). Finally, by the end of the Civil War, districts appointed superintendents who then appointed principals for administration and accountability. Although boards assessed the effectiveness and efficiency of schools with achievement tests, the results were not made public for political leverage (Cuban, 2004). The results were used instead to direct instruction.

By the end of World War I, achievement tests were commonly used in school districts nationwide. The 1950s were shaken by two important events that ushered in a new era of federal intervention into the heretofore local and state control of education (Finn, 2008). In 1954, the Supreme Court *Brown* decision outlawed segregation in schools. The consequence of that decision required that federal rule would become a presence in school operations that continues today. Then in 1957, the Soviet Union launched *Sputnik*. Fear that Americans were falling behind in the space race prompted the National Defense Education Act to assign federal funds for math, science, and foreign languages. With the federal funds, a new level of accountability followed, and local schools and states began to feel the heavy hand of federal oversight. By 1965, the emphasis of school accountability changed from efficiency and effective use and services access to a focus on student outcomes with the enactment of the Elementary and Secondary Education Act (ESEA) of 1965 (Beadie, 2004; Cuban, 2004).

The ESEA was enacted as a part of President Johnson's "War on Poverty." Title I, the largest and perhaps the most important of the five titles that comprise this law, is a program of federal funding currently touching fifty thousand schools and seventeen million students nationwide from preschool through high school (U.S. Department of Education, Title I: Improving Basic Programs). Equity and excellence rely upon assisting children in poverty who are identified as at risk of dropping out. ESEA and the federal role in American education have since continued to expand to the current Title I program (U.S. Department of Education, 2010). In 2001, the federal program was renamed No Child Left Behind. The political climate at the time was largely influenced by the belief that schools were failing our nation's children. One cannot discuss or examine high-stakes accountability without acknowledging the political winds that were whipped into a fury by the controversial study *A Nation at Risk* (U.S. Department of Education, 1983).

In 1981, the secretary of education, T. H. Bell, appointed the National Commission on Excellence in Education with a charge to report on the quality of education in America. The resulting report, *A Nation at Risk*, fueled the school reform movement and prepared the way for the age of accountability. The report concluded, "The educational foundations of our society are presently being eroded by a rising tide of mediocrity that threatens our very future as a Nation and a people" (U.S. Department of Education, 1983, p. 9). In other words, our schools were failing in their job, and our nation was in danger of losing its role as an international leader and world power.

The report asserted that the call for excellence and educational reform must not "be made at the expense of a strong public commitment to the equitable treatment of our diverse population" (U.S. Department of Education, 1983, p. 14). Reading between the lines and knowing the racial tension in the climate of the times, it was generally perceived that school integration and an increasing level of poverty in schools were the causes for the erosion of educational excellence and the consequent state of mediocrity. Later, in a speech to the National Association for the Advancement of Colored People (NAACP) given in 2000, George Bush again brought this concern to our attention when he called the issue the "soft bigotry of low expectations" for children of poverty and diversity.

A Nation at Risk ushered in the era of accountability. Today, this significant report still warrants study by educational leaders in order to fully appreciate its emotional and consequent policy impact. The report was charged with highly emotional language that served its persuasive intent more powerfully than the data it relayed. *A Nation at Risk* placed the major responsibility for the dangerous state of affairs squarely on the shoulders of educators. The report compelled the nation to fix schools in "four important aspects of the educational process: content, expectations, time, and teaching" (U.S. Department of Education, 1983, p. 17). Politicians led the hue and cry to reform schools that struck a strong emotional chord of public sentiment. It is a chord that both political parties strike as often as votes are needed. And consequently, often it has been one of the few places where bipartisanship has been able to operate.

Politics and political agendas permeate the topic of accountability. The impetus for school reform and accountability is thrust forward by the power of political agendas. *A Nation at Risk* painted a bleak picture of public schools that was intended to strengthen the case for vouchers and to support private schools, but instead it has resulted in increased federal funding for public schools from $16 billion in 1983 to $70 billion in the budget request for 2013. Our nation invests heavily in our schools and consequently calls for accountability through improved student performance.

WHAT IS HAPPENING?

Although the principle purpose of this chapter is not an argument for or against high-stakes accountability testing, it is critical to analyze the student performance results since the implementation of NCLB. Current punitive measures imply that failure to meet standards is an act of will because educators and students aren't trying hard enough! The policies operate within the mindset of a behaviorist model that advocates for punishment and reward as the most effective means to change behavior. This reasoning concludes that if consequences for failure are harsh enough, success will result (Beadie, 2004). The threat is "improved scores or else!" Has this high-stakes pressure achieved its intent? Are we reaching the goals set by NCLB?

NCLB Student Performance Goals

Before examining the data on student performance, a brief reminder of the NCLB performance goals is important. There are four pillars of NCLB, enacted in 2002. This study focuses on the first and most significant pillar of NCLB mandating increased accountability for student performance in five areas: state standards, assessment system, accountability system, adequate yearly progress, and school improvement. NCLB requires states to develop standards for curriculum (knowledge and skills) and to set achievement standards aligned to the state curriculum along with an aligned assessment instrument that measures student achievement. As a result, each state has developed its own curriculum, its own assessment instrument, and its subsequent standards on that assessment. The assessments are then tied to the sanctions and rewards of an accountability system and a national system for measuring Adequate Yearly Progress (AYP).

Failing to meet AYP for two consecutive years puts schools into the five levels of School Improvement. Being identified for School Improvement is an unhappy situation. Year 1 sanctions include providing parents with school choice to transfer from the school in question. The most severe sanctions come in year 4, which requires restructure, and year 5 requires implementation of an alternative governance or takeover. It takes two years of meeting AYP to leave the School Improvement status.

Schools are the heartbeat of communities, and being designated for School Improvement can be devastating to the pride of the school and community stakeholders and the economy of the district. With or without sanctions, AYP puts administrator jobs on the line. In turn, administrators pressure the faculty, and then the faculty pressures students! At the heart of this pressure is data. The statistics from high-stakes tests serve as the hammer for school improvement. In the following section, this study examines the statistics that should be clear and unquestionable. However, as Mark Twain once said, "There are three types of lies: lies, damned lies, and statistics!" What we know is that analysis of empirical data can come to opposite conclusions based on the philosophical and political positions of the reporter.

Adequate Yearly Progress

AYP is the first and strongest measurement for school accountability. AYP is simply defined as the progress schools need to make each year in order to reach 100 percent passing rate on the state-designed high-stakes assessments by 2014. AYP also highlights the progress of demographic groups and special populations with this same measure. The assessment instruments and standards vary from state to state, which explains a major difficulty that researchers have in analyzing and comparing the national data from AYP: one national AYP accountability system but fifty different state curriculums, assessments, and standards.

Despite the comparability issues, the Center on Education Policy estimated 49 percent of the schools in our nation did not make AYP in 2011 (based on state reports to the U.S. Department of Education; Usher, 2012). That number is a significant increase from 29 percent in 2006. This data is even more dramatic when one realizes that many were able to escape failure by appealing for special exemptions. With the startling number of schools failing to meet AYP, the need for reforming NCLB has resulted in states applying for waivers to avoid the consequences that loom before them as the 2014 100 percent deadline approaches. According to the U.S. Department of Education, as of September 10, 2012, thirty-three states had NCLB waivers approved. Although AYP provides a muddy picture of the student performance and the effectiveness of school reform, schools are still facing the clear threat of failure according to its measure. Fortunately, valid and reliable data are available to answer our questions about improved student performance since NCLB included National Assessment of Educational Progress (NAEP) assessments into the data collection system. By examining the student performance on this nationally standardized test, we can have a clear picture of student achievement progress across the nation.

National Assessment of Educational Progress

National Assessment of Educational Progress (NAEP), the largest national assessment of student academic progress, is run by the Commission of Education Statistics, with the National Center for Education Statistics, in the U.S. Department of Education (NAEP, 2012, section 3). This standardized test has served as a common measurement of student achievement in math and reading since 1969, and longitudinal data are available since 1971. Consequently, it is a reliable measure of national student progress within the limitations of standardized testing. NCLB requires states receiving Title I funds to administer NAEP to a sampling of students in the fourth and eighth grades. States must comply, but there is neither award nor sanction for performance on this national standardized student assessment. The annual NAEP assessments use a stratified random sampling to identify those tested. Consequently, the data is both reliable and valid for comparability studies to evaluate student progress in the United States, as opposed to the wide variance in state assessments used to gauge AYP.

The executive summary of the "Nation's Report Card" (NAEP, 2008) shows the performance data in math and reading since 1971 until 2008. NAEP reading scores for all students since 1971 show a twelve-point average gain for nine-year-olds and a four-point average gain for thirteen-year-olds. NAEP math scores from 1973 until 2008 for nine-year-olds showed a twenty-four-point increase, and thirteen-year-olds saw an average score increase by fifteen points. In contrast, the average scores for seventeen-year-olds showed no significant difference over that same period.

According to the executive summary, racial/ethnic group scores show that although the performance gaps between black and white have been narrowed since 1971, there was no significant change from 2004 to 2008. The same was true for the Hispanic and white gap. So although average scores were generally higher, the gaps remained consistent. It is interesting to note that once again there was no performance change for seventeen-year-olds.

Further scrutiny of the progress of students on the NAEP since the implementation of NCLB yields little or no significant increase in the math or reading scores in all age groups. Younger students have made the greatest average performance improvement on both reading and math. Thirteen-year-olds showed modest improvement, while the performance trends for seventeen-year-olds remains relatively flat.

So we ask ourselves the question again: has the high-stakes accountability testing of this accountability era raised student performance in schools? And the answer is, yes? no? maybe? The answer often depends upon point of view, since "assessing student achievement is a matter of inference" (Mabry, 2004, p. 121). Looking at the longitudinal data since 1971, one can definitely see improvement in student performance on the standardized test. In 2009, the secretary of education and the U.S. Department of Education published a report likewise demonstrating a very positive perspective on the same data that we have just viewed. Yes, indeed, the scores today are the highest in decades. Exposing student performance to public view has prompted a sharpened focus on curriculum and instruction. It has done what assessment is designed to do—inform instruction.

However, refocusing our examination of NAEP data since the enactment of NCLB shows more modest gains. Consequently, one might question if high-stakes accountability sanctions have been very effective. Rather than let a political group or a representative of a philosophical ideology give the answer, leaders should come to conclusions for themselves. There is truth in every answer. Schools must accept the singular truth and reality that accountability and high-stakes testing will be with us for a long time yet. Finally, there are consequences that cannot be ignored with that reality.

WHERE ARE WE GOING?

"Testing values measurement and quantification, and objectivity over subjectivity. . . the testing community places little value on the many social, cultural and individual factors that also influence how a student performs on a test" (Madaus & Russell, 2010–2011, p. 22). This statement reminds us that the subjects of the tests are humans, rich in variety and differences. Achievement, intelligence, and aptitude cannot be weighed like a pound of butter or measured like a yard of fabric. Test scores should not be evaluated in isolation. To do so provides invalid results, since validity is found in multiple measures (Mabry, 2004).

> Does anyone seriously believe that what a kid scores on an on-demand test really represents anything more than a small sample of highly contextualized paper-and-pencil behavior, ostensibly having something to do with teaching and learning, and these days a lot to do with a heavy dose of test preparation? Surely, what matters more is the cumulative impact of teaching and learning and the future potential of each child and young adult in the care of public schools. (Sirotnik, 2004, p. 8)

We are entangled in the good intentions behind measuring student performance with high-stakes accountability testing and the unintended consequences of threat. Can we reconcile the paradoxes that are seen in the conflicting intended outcomes and unintended consequences? Educators who understand the power of brain-enriched environments and brain-compatible instruction can resolve the conflict.

Understanding the Consequences

Much has been written about the negative effects of high-stakes testing, although little significant empirical research has emerged from the debate. Policy makers highly regard empirical, scientific studies that come from the standardized testing data, but investigating the issues of unintended consequences oftentimes finds studies qualitative in nature and limited in scope. So what educators see and understand from everyday implementation of high-stakes testing accountability is largely discounted by policy makers.

This chapter does not aim to argue the substance of any claim. For example, some point to increased dropouts with high-stakes testing.

Teachers and administrators can share anecdotal stories of students who dropped out because they could not pass the test. Even though data from the National Center for Educational Statistics show a declining trend in dropouts, when you tease out the differences between event dropout rate, status dropout rate, and average freshman graduation rate, a different picture is presented (Chapman, Laird, Ifill, & KewalRamani, 2011). The freshman graduation rate (the percentage of freshmen who graduate within four years) is considered a reliable completion indicator, but the longitudinal data using this measure is not available to analyze the specific impact of NCLB. This National Center for Educational Statistics report does show that the current national average freshman graduation rate for 2009 was 75.5 percent, one percentage point higher than in 2008 at 74.9 percent (Chapman et al., 2011). Although the data shows that race, sex, and socioeconomic factors were contributors to dropouts and freshman completers, one cannot infer from the data what role high-stakes testing played in these figures. However, alarmed educators know the math. A 75 percent completion rate means that 25 percent of the students who began the ninth grade did not finish four years later. In schools these are not just percentages; they are real numbers that represent real students—children of our community. When do the numbers matter? If one student drops out because of testing, it matters.

Additionally, others point to cheating as another negative consequence of the high-stakes testing accountability. Cheating scandals from Atlanta to Philadelphia and from New York to Florida cross our nation. With each scandal, a public outcry is heard, but how many more go unreported? Again, our data of anecdotal incidences does not provide empirical evidence that cheating has increased with high-stakes testing. However, educators see and know what the data does not show.

Reconciling the Conflict

Leave the arguments behind. Bring the children forward and teach them well. Inoculate them from the negative consequences with brain-compatible instruction. Instruction should be about the individual child. For most educators, the intent of NCLB is more than a philosophy; it is a conviction and commitment. It will never be acceptable to leave any child behind.

In contrast, a brain-enriched environment ignores the distractions of the debate in order to focus on the whole student. Teach them well! If a student is a strong reader, then the reading test loses its threat. The principles of brain-compatible instruction give us a way to counter the unintended consequences of the heavy-handed sanctions. Furthermore, it is easy for the public to forget that in order for students to perform at their best, educators must also be high performers. Educators need brain-compatible learning, too! How can we be a learning community when we are only fighting to survive? So we begin by looking to the same principles of brain compatibility for teachers and administrators. In schools, learning is not just for students; teachers and administrators are the first learners in this community. Without proper training and tools to meet instructional challenges in high-stakes accountability testing, teachers and administrators are threatened and fearful. Fear of failure for themselves and their students and a threat to career and livelihood push educators to downshift from thinking and reasoning to survival mode—fight or flight.

Knowledge and skills can beat back fear. Providing educators with professional development for creating brain-enriched environments and supporting them by using brain-compatible principles empowers teachers to reject the negative consequences to which many have fallen prey. Brain compatibility offers an exciting possibility for educators. We can optimize the learning capacity for our students by creating the natural and brain-enriched environment. Better learners learn more!

Natural and Brain-Enriched Learning Environments

This chapter presents a limited perspective of the rich world of scholarship* written on brain research and natural learning by focusing on select concepts important to the science. First, and most importantly, safe environments are necessary for optimal learning. Second, the brain is a system that grows and changes in the learning process as it searches for meaning and relevance. Significant learning happens through experience and developing connections. Third, the social brain learns best in communities. And fourth, a brain-enriched environment respects learning differences.

Remove Threat

Safe schools and safe classrooms remove both physical and psychological threats. Fear is a strong emotion. When in danger, the brain downshifts into instinctive behaviors of fight and flight where learning does not happen. Low-performing campuses and at-risk students are the most likely victims to know fear of failure. These students often come without the confidence of success, and fearful educators reinforce their insecurities by focusing on the student inadequacies. The brain protects itself, grows, and changes to survive in the world it finds itself. A brain-enriched environment removes physical threats and needs of hunger, comfort, and bodily harm. There are, however, subtler and less obvious threats to self-esteem, pride, and emotional harm. The school must first be a safe place for all learners—students and educators.

Make Meaning

The brain works in concert with the body and mind. Every experience and event impacts the brain. Growing dendrites and making new brain connections increases intelligence. The brain learns by searching for meaning through patterns that make connections to prior experiences. With those patterns we build mental models that shape our understanding of the world. Since the brain seeks and needs to make connections, information or activities in isolation without connection have no meaning. The search for meaning is innate. Each one of us is born to learn by striving to make sense of the world in which we live. We are programmed to question and search—to learn. Instruction in a brain-enriched classroom encourages questioning by providing new and interesting experiences to prompt students to search for meaning.

Unfortunately, fearful educators narrow the curriculum by attempting to teach only that which is tested. Again, the most fragile students suffer the most without the richness of experience and content. Other students get experience and connections outside of school at home with family and activities. Brain enrichment provides secure foundations for learners to reach beyond and make new and meaningful connections. Concepts are central to meaningful and relevant learning that is transferable because they provide the umbrella to cover and connect ideas and facts. Without relevance and meaning, instruction is wasted and lost.

How much of schooling is meaningless for our students? Empowered teachers using brain-compatible learning principles increase learning for students by building on strengths and making connections through rich experiences that provide learning successes. These instructors create excitement and interest to motivate learners. Fragile students need empowered, confident teachers. This principle gives educators hope when working with children from at-risk environments, as well as weighing them with the grave responsibility to monitor what comes into the physical and emotional world of these learners.

Build Community

Learning happens best with and through others because the brain is social. Brain-enriched learning environments support and nurture community. Optimal learning is language rich. Collaborative learning activities, invitation to dialogue, and discussion feed the social brain. All students profit, but the at-risk students gain the most.

Respect Differences

Finally, a brain-enriched environment recognizes the individual differences while understanding the universal principle of brain/learning processes. The accountability system and high-stakes testing work on a factory model that monitors consistent material input and expects a product that meets standard expectations. Unfortunately, children and brains do not fit this model. It takes courageous educators and school leaders to protect children from the conveyor-belt harm that the system invokes. The best protection is optimizing their learning potential. Providing a brain-enriched learning environment is the best test preparation.

RESOLUTION

Schools will need to continue to prepare themselves and their students for continued high-stakes accountability testing. Even with the proposed reformed reauthorization for ESEA, assessment of student performance remains the central measurement of school success. Schools will still need to focus attention on all demographic groups to work toward equity and excellence. We will not be able to hide our shortcomings in the average or overall success of the majority. These intended outcomes are good. A valuable exercise for beleaguered faculty members and administrators is to take the time to count their blessings with accountability. There are many intended outcomes that are valuable for all schools and their students. However, every school needs to prepare itself to counter the unintended negative consequences that will ensue. The primary reason for the negative consequences is fear—fear for jobs, fear for reputations, fear of failure, and fear for children. While some rise to the challenge, too many educators have downshifted into the fight or flight mode. The results are often very disheartening. Educators can meet the challenge of high-stakes assessments with high-capacity learners.

Developing policy for positive educational progress is slow and oftentimes misguided. Former U.S. Department of Education official Chester Finn lamented, "I saw how clumsy and weak are Washington's instruments for effecting changes in education; how seemingly good ideas, once translated into legislation and bureaucracy, often end up not working; how much easier it is even near the pinnacle of government, to prevaricate, argue, and block change than to accomplish things; yet also how steady goals and perseverance can matter over the long haul" (2008, p. 68).

Bureaucrats are too busy with bureaucracy and power struggles among special interest groups. However, we still need reasonable and informed voices to contribute to policy making and call for "responsible assessment and accountability" to be conducted in a way that promotes "educational aims and ideals" (Sigel, 2004, p. 63). School and community leaders must insist their voices be heard over the din of politics and special interests because the most important special interest for our nation is the well-being of students.

In the meantime, consultants are making money on materials and workshops. Packaged curriculums with a promise of alignment to standards and test preparation are big business. Administrators search for the silver bullet through products and services in a desperate attempt to keep their jobs. Superintendents and principals turn over at the speed of assessment data to be replaced by someone who can convince school boards they can transform a school—in other words, raise scores. Everyone is at risk: teachers, administrators, and elected officials, but most of all students.

Educators should be reminded of Franklin Roosevelt's famous words: "The only thing we have to fear is fear itself." We have the knowledge and skills available at our fingertips to become courageous, but educational leaders must lead the charge. Apply the brain-compatible principles of learning to develop faculties and administrators first. Create the brain-enriched environment and empower educators with brain-compatible instructional knowledge and skills.

REFERENCES

Beadie, N. (2004). Moral errors and strategic mistakes: Lessons from the history of student accountability. In K. A. Sirotnik (Ed.), *Holding accountability accountable: What ought to matter in public education* (pp. 35–50). New York: Teachers College Press.

Chapman, C., Laird, L., Ifill, N., & KewalRamani, A. (2011). Trends in high school dropout and completion rates in the United States: 1972–2009. National Center for Educational Statistics Publication No. 2012006. Retrieved from http://nces.ed.gov/ccd/pub_dropouts.asp.

Cuban, L. (2004). Looking through the rearview mirror at school accountability. In K. A. Sirotnik (Ed.), *Holding accountability accountable: What ought to matter in public education* (pp. 18–34). New York: Teachers College Press.

Dictionary.com. (n.d.). Accountability. Retrieved from http://dictionary.reference.com/browse/accountability.

Finn, C. E., Jr. (2008). *Troublemaker: A personal history of school reform since Sputnik*. Princeton, NJ: Princeton University Press.

Mabry, L. (2004). Strange yet familiar: Assessment-driven education. In K. A. Sirotnik (Ed.), *Holding accountability accountable: What ought to matter in public education* (pp. 116–134). New York: Teachers College Press.

Madaus, G., & Russell, M. (2010–2011). Paradoxes of high-stakes testing. *Journal of Education, 190*(1/2), 21–30. Retrieved from http://www.bu.edu/journalofeducation.

National Assessment of Educational Progress (NAEP); (2012). NAEP overview. Retrieved from http://nces.ed.gov/nationsreportcard/about.

National Assessment of Educational Progress (NAEP); (2008). The nation's report card: Executive summary. Retrieved from http://nationsreportcard.gov/ltt_2008/ltt0001.asp.

Sigel, H. (2004). What ought to matter in public schooling: Judgment, standards, and responsible accountability. In K. A. Sirotnik (Ed.), *Holding accountability accountable: What ought to matter in public education* (pp. 51–65). New York: Teachers College Press.

Sirotnik, K. A. (Ed.). (2004). *Holding accountability accountable: What ought to matter in public education*. New York: Teachers College Press.

U.S. Department of Education. (2012). The federal role in education. Retrieved from http://www.ed.gov/about/overview/fed/role.html?src=ln.

U.S. Department of Education. National Commission on Excellence in Education. (1983). *A nation at risk: The imperative for educational reform.* Washington, DC: Author. Retrieved from http://datacenter.spps.org/uploads/SOTW_A_Nation_at_Risk_1983.pdf.

U.S. Department of Education. Office of the Secretary, Margaret Spellings. (2009). Great expectations: Holding ourselves and our schools accountable for results (executive summary). Retrieved from http://www2.ed.gov/nclb/overview/importance/greatexpectations/index.html.

Usher, A. (2012). AYP results for 2012-11-May 2012 update. George Washington University Center on Education Policy. Retrieved from http://www.cep-dc.org/displayDocument.cfm?DocumentID=403.

*My own learning journey took a dramatic turn when I was teaching ninth-grade English and studied with a writing project that introduced me to *Making Connections: Teaching and the Human Brain*, by Geoffrey and Renate Caine (see chapter 3). I call that my "Damascus road experience" because it changed my teaching life. I continued to learn from their future writings, as well from work by Eric Jensen, Leslie Hart, Patricia Wolfe, and others. I owe a huge debt of gratitude to their work and the opportunities I had to participate in workshops and trainings on brain-compatible learning throughout my career as a teacher, educational consultant, and principal. Although they are not listed in the references, they are the source of my knowledge and understanding, as well as my passion for brain-compatible instruction and brain-enriched environment in schools.

Chapter Three

The Brain/Mind Principles of Natural Learning

Renate N. Caine and Geoffrey Caine

What's important now is that 21st century educators should take the position that an educational product that doesn't emerge out of an exploratory process isn't worth assessing. It's appalling how much energy many schools currently spend on memorized preparations to meet politicized product standards. It's such a contradiction: a wealthy society that's very thankful for the creativity that sparked contemporary society is now seemingly uninterested in developing even more creative folks.

—Robert Sylwester (2012)

A blend of research from neuroscience and the various branches of psychology is literally rewriting our collective understanding of learning. So much so that it would be a mistake for educators to simply integrate this research into a model of teaching that still largely emphasizes transmission and memorization. When taken seriously, brain/mind research challenges deeply held assumptions about the way that schooling and teaching are defined and are generally done. The Brain/Mind Learning Principles, our synthesis of the research that we first formulated in 1991 (Caine & Caine, 1991, 1994) and continuously update (Caine, Caine, McClintic, & Klimek, 2009), go far beyond the direct instruction all too frequently required by the system and tied to success on tests.

That can be challenging. The two of us often find ourselves in workshops with large groups of teachers, exploring the Brain/Mind Learning Principles. The purpose of the workshops is to expand everyone's view of the many ways in which human beings learn.

Teachers usually find both the information and ideas fascinating—until we ask them to look at how this information can inform their own teaching. At this point teachers become both confused and puzzled. The bridge between this solid research and their own teaching practice simply seems not to be there. We had to search deeper in order to understand what was happening. The problem turns out to be more about their own beliefs, thinking, and habits—all of which are deeply entrenched—and the many through which they were perceiving and interpreting our ideas.

THE EDUCATION MEME

In our latest book (Caine & Caine, 2011) we expose this educational paradigm as a "meme," a word coined by the biologist Richard Dawkins. A meme is an organized way of thinking tied to action based on a powerful belief about how the world works, one that is shared by a very large number of individuals. It is so taken for granted that it seems to have taken on a life of its own. In the case of education, there is a meme, a set of powerful beliefs so strong that they are preventing new ideas from taking hold. For example, let's take the question "what does it mean to learn in school?" In our experience, the vast majority of adults who are asked this question will insist that success requires a textbook, prescribed content, and teacher-controlled instruction guided by assignments, homework, and tests. When so many adults identify the same elements without prompting, we are looking at a meme.

- Parents expect to see teacher-assigned homework, grades, and tests; unions want to tie teacher time spent in front of the classroom as work that creates "learning" and earned pay.
- Politicians too look at direct instruction tied to teacher action and ultimately to test scores, all based on beliefs about school, teaching, and what it means to learn.
- Similarly, ask students in any class why they are studying what they are studying, and after looking at you as though you are a bit mad, they will respond that they are doing it because their teacher told them to do it or because they have to do it in order to pass a test or get a grade. Their own motivation, enthusiasm, and effort to find unique solutions to per-

sonally relevant questions are rarely engaged. (The same incidentally holds true for teachers forced to teach the standards using standardized instruction.) The governing meme keeps everyone from questioning what is being done.

Shifting the meme for education begins with a richer understanding of how human beings learn naturally. Is brain-based learning and even "neuroeducation" really new? The point is that both could be revolutionary if it were not for the old meme. As it is, powerful research continues to be reduced to what everyone understands schools and schooling to look like.

This new research reveals a more complex view of what it means to learn, one that includes the role of emotions, higher-order thinking, social relationships, the physical environment, state of mind, and more. Many scholars have come to the conclusion, based on the emerging convergence of so much research, that each person should be regarded as a unique, integrated living system (Fuster, 2003; Damasio, 2005). Some educators intuitively understand this as they experience their students as complex and "whole" individuals every day in their classrooms. The entire organism—the whole person—interacts with its world. When we see sophisticated research showing that body, brain, heart, and mind are all involved in learning, the real job of the teacher becomes more visible and the call for alternative ways of teaching becomes more justified. The old meme does not address the many complex social and emotional issues that confront teachers every day.

Helping students "learn" from the perspective of the brain/mind leads to an entirely new vision of what it means to work toward mastery, a process that we now call natural learning. Here are some examples:

- Research on neural plasticity shows that the brain is extraordinarily malleable and that many areas of the cortex are literally shaped by experience (Begley, 2007; Conlan, 1999; Diamond & Hobson, 1988; Doige, 2007).
- Research on the vast degree of interconnectedness between different regions of the brain, and on the nature of neural networks, indicates that academic learning and comprehension is never separate from emotions, meaning, motivation, past experience, recognition, and memory (Fuster, 2003).

- Research on what are called "mirror neurons" demonstrates that children are social beings and continuously and largely unconsciously learn from what is modeled by others around them (Iacoboni et al., 1999; Rizzolatti & Sinigaglia, 2006).
- Research on emotions and the brain confirms that some types of comprehending are inhibited by fear and helplessness (LeDoux, 1996; Wiedenfeld et al., 1990), and it shows how the more positive emotions can affect and enhance certain types of learning (Panksepp, 1998; Peterson, Maier, & Seligman, 1995).

We realized how critical this emergent research could be for educators. Yet we also recognized that this information had little chance of getting to teachers and administrators given the focus of their past professional development and the intensity of their day-to-day classroom responsibilities. So the goal of our writing, including this chapter, is to help educators to rewrite the traditional view of instruction in schools. Specifically, this chapter will highlight the following:

- Basic learning principles that impact learning and comprehension
- A process that helps teachers translate the principles into practice
- An introduction to a model of teaching that most readily parallels natural learning and teaching in a technologically rich world. We call this approach to teaching the Guided Experience Approach.

What's Out There Today: Established Research and Practice

In the late 1980s we began to integrate research from neuroscience, perceptual psychology, behaviorism, cognitive psychology, biology, and a large number of other fields. The result was a set of Brain/Mind Learning Principles, which are updated and expanded, continuously sparked by new and ongoing research (Caine et al., 2009). The principles are grounded in the view of human beings as living systems and have to meet four basic criteria:

1. The phenomena described by a principle should be universal. A Brain/Mind Learning Principle must be true for all human beings, despite individual genetic variations, unique experiences, and developmental differences.

2. Research documenting any one specific principle should be evidenced in, and its influence must span, more than one field or discipline. Since a learning principle describes a system's property, one would expect it to be validated and confirmed by triangulation of research that crosses multiple fields and disciplines.

3. A principle should anticipate future research. It should be expected and anticipated that research will continue to emerge that refines and confirms each learning principle. For example, much of the current brain research on the links between emotion and cognition was published after we first formulated our principles in 1991. Thus a principle is a continuous work in progress, in the sense that new, ongoing research is constantly shaping and advancing our understanding of each truth a principle addresses.

4. The principle should provide implications for practice. By their nature, principles are so general that they cannot be expected to tell educators precisely what to do. However, effective learning principles ought, as a minimum, to provide the basis for an effective general framework to guide decisions about teaching and help in the identification and selection of appropriate methods and strategies. Principles illuminate new sparks of capacities for learning, which can be translated into further enhancements of instructional practices.

BRAIN/MIND PRINCIPLES OF NATURAL LEARNING

The principles do not follow a sequential or hierarchical pattern. While each principle reveals a capacity that all students have for learning, comprehending, and mastery, they work together. It is in this coherence and integration that they provide a deeper understanding of what it means to teach to so much potential.

Principle 1: All Learning Engages the Physiology

One reason so much traditional teaching involves students sitting in their assigned seats is the belief that the brain is somehow separate from the body and that the body is not very involved in learning. The research on neural plasticity, as well as other research, tells us that the body and mind are totally interconnected (Capra, 1996; Damasio, 1994; Diamond &

Hobson, 1998; Gibbs, 2007). Cognitive scientists often refer to this in terms of embodied cognition (see, e.g., Lakoff & Johnson, 1999; Robson, 2011) or the embodied mind (Varela, Thompson & Rosch, 1991). The brain is a parallel processor in which body, emotions, senses, memory, motivation, and action are deeply interconnected and activated simultaneously.

Capacity 1

All students have the capacity to comprehend more effectively when involved in experiences that naturally call on the use of their senses and their bodies.

Principle 2: The Brain/Mind Is Social

Every individual on this planet comes complete with what Alison Gopnik, Andrew Meltzoff, and Patricia Kuhl (1999) have called the "contact urge." Healthy social relationships, with an emphasis on belonging, being recognized, listened to, and noticed, all contribute to an optimal state of mind we call "relaxed alertness" (Cozolino, 2013; Goleman, 2006; Sternberg & Grigorenko, 2001). Recent research on mirror neurons confirms that the social nature of human beings is grounded in biology (Cozolino, 2013). The social nature of learning is sometimes described in terms of situated learning (see, e.g., Lave & Wenger, 1991).

Capacity 2

All students have the capacity to comprehend more effectively when their needs for social interactions and relationship are engaged and honored.

Principle 3: The Search for Meaning Is Innate

The need to make sense of things is characteristic of every human being from infancy to adulthood. It has been called the "explanatory drive" (Gopnik, Meltzoff, & Kuhl, 1999). One aspect of even young students' search for meaning is illustrated by the way that all people respond to novelty. Here is an example: in reading a text on one of Christopher Columbus's voyages, imagine yourself as a rat on the ship. What is your point of view of the voyage?

Another dimension of the mind's innate search for meaning has to do with the compelling power of purpose (Hillman, 1996). For example, a girl of about nine years old recently described what she understood to be the causes and best treatment for breast cancer. She was extremely articulate. Her interest had been sparked by the fact that her mother had been diagnosed with the disease, prompting her to read as much as she could find on the subject. Learning that is reducible to memorizing facts that are true or false is different from learning that engages actor-centered, adaptive decision making (Goldberg, 2001). This kind of decision making is the result of an authentic question generated by the learner on the basis of a genuine need to know and is one that inevitably requires more complex thinking. It is the search for meaning that organizes actor-centered questions and encourages the use of higher-order functions.

Capacity 3

All students have the capacity to comprehend more effectively when their interests, purposes, and ideas are engaged and honored.

Principle 4: The Search for Meaning Occurs through Patterning

Patterning refers to the meaningful organization and categorization of information. People make sense of experience by their mind's drive to find and create patterns and relationships. The brain is designed to perceive and generate patterns and resists having meaningless patterns imposed on it by others. Cognitive scientists have developed a large number of terms in order to describe patterning, terms such as categories, frames, and schemata. All decision making before, during, and after an experience is based on the patterns that people perceive and the choices that are made about where to focus their attention. Education should be about increasing the patterns students can use, recognize, and communicate to gain new knowledge and ideas (Restak, 2001; Shermer, 2008).

Capacity 4

All students have substantial unused capacities to perceive and create patterns and to link those new patterns to what they already understand.

Principle 5: Emotions Are Critical to Patterning

Emotions are central to human life. Neuroscience now shows that emotions are involved in every thought, decision, and response (Damasio, 1999; Pert 1997; Pessoa, 2008). Powerful learning is enhanced by rich emotional experiences, which are guided and moderated by higher-order functions. In fact, emotion and physical reactions are so much a part of understanding that psychologist Eugene Gendlin (1982) describes the link in terms of the phrase "felt meaning."

Capacity 5

All students can comprehend more effectively when appropriate emotions are elicited before, during, and after their engagement with meaningful experiences.

Principle 6: The Brain/Mind Processes Parts and Wholes Simultaneously

The brain/mind is designed to make sense of the world. Making sense of experience requires both a big picture and paying attention to the individual parts and details. The experience of the whole provides a story, a model, or a fascinating example of what can be achieved. Gestalt psychology explicitly shows how the mind connects parts to make these wholes (Sternberg, 2008). And some of the most recent brain research is now exploring this relationship between parts and wholes in terms of neural networks—lattices of individual neurons that fire together to represent knowledge and experience (Fuster, 2003).

Capacity 6

All students can comprehend more effectively when details (specific facts and information) are embedded in wholes that they understand such as a real-life event, a meaningful story, or a project that they create or witness.

Principle 7: Learning Involves Both Focused Attention and Peripheral Perception

Every human being is continuously immersed in a field of stimuli and constantly selects a part of that field to attend to. Attention is a natural phenomenon guided by interest, novelty, emotion, and meaning, and paying attention is critical. What is less understood is the fact that human beings also learn from the background—the context that is not consciously attended to. This is illustrated by research on implicit memory (Schacter, 1996), as well as mirror neurons (Rizzolatti & Sinigaglia, 2006), which shows how children "pick up" behaviors, beliefs, and preferences or dislikes while engaging in life experience.

Capacity 7

All students can comprehend more effectively when their attention is deepened and multiple layers of the context are used to support learning.

Principle 8: Learning Is Both Conscious and Unconscious

Learning involves layers of consciousness. Some learning requires a person to consciously attend to a problem that needs to be solved or analyzed. Some learning at a deeper level requires unconscious incubation in the same way that the creative insights of artists and scientists sometimes occur after the mind has done some conscious processing. Beyond that, really successful students are also capable of monitoring themselves by means of the executive functions of their brains (Denkla, 1999; Hurley, 2006)—a central feature of higher-order functions—so that they know their own strengths and weaknesses and can take charge of how they process experience.

Capacity 8

All students can comprehend more effectively when given time to reflect on and process those experiences about which they live, read, and view.

Principle 9: There Are at Least Two Approaches to Memory

Researchers have identified many different memory systems. These tend to be organized into two primary categories: declarative and procedural memories. However, of more value to educators in our view is the separation of memories in a slightly different way (e.g., O'Keefe & Nadel, 1978); educators need to make this separation and understand that it is between rote memorization, which is the hallmark of traditional approaches to teaching, and the dynamic memory that is engaged in everyday experience. Sometimes facts or steps in strategies do need to be memorized, but rote learning is different from dynamic memory. Dynamic memory is likely to be engaged naturally as learners sift through the ideas that they recognize in order to make sense of new contexts.

Capacity 9

All students can master material more effectively when multiple memory systems are engaged simultaneously.

Principle 10: Learning Is Developmental

All human beings develop in several somewhat predictable ways, though they rarely master anything in precisely the same way or at exactly the same rate. There are stages in brain development, for instance, and in the formation of identity, all of which impact comprehension (Bransford, Brown, & Cocking, 2000; Sylwester, 2007). In addition, all learning builds on previous learning. We now know that this additive/cumulative process is accompanied by changes in the physiology of the brain (Huttenlocher, 2002). This mental alteration is, in turn, altered by new experiences, and the cycle continues throughout life. Unfortunately, the traditional age/grade organization of students does not adequately deal with the realities of mental, emotional, or social development. Performance, not age or grade level, provides a much better foundation for teaching.

Capacity 10

All students can comprehend more effectively if individual differences in maturation, development, and prior learning are taken into consideration.

Principle 11: Complex Learning Is Enhanced by Challenge and Inhibited by Threat Associated with Helplessness and Fatigue

A great deal of research from such disciplines as neuroscience (e.g., Cozolino, 2013; LeDoux, 1996), creativity theory (Deci & Ryan, 1985,

2002), stress theory (Cozolino, 2013; Lazarus, 1999; Sapolsky, 1998), and perceptual psychology (Combs, 1999) shows that effective mental functioning can be sabotaged by fears associated with helplessness. Thus, meaningful learning can be sabotaged. One consequence of such frightening negative emotions is that higher-order executive functioning have been hijacked (Lazarus, 1999). That is why the optimal state of mind for higher-order thinking and learning is relaxed alertness, a combination of low threat and high intrinsic challenge.

Capacity 11

All students can comprehend more effectively in a supportive, empowering, and challenging environment.

Principle 12: Each Brain Is Uniquely Organized

The paradox that faces education is that human beings are both similar and different. For example, every human being is an expression of DNA. Yet every individual has a unique genetic blueprint. Everyone has a lifetime of experience, and yet some of the experiences of every person are unique. All of this complexity is compounded by a wide variety of social, ethnic, gender, and economic differences (e.g., Gardner, 2006; Myers-Briggs Type Indicator, http://www.myersbriggs.org/).

Capacity 12

All students can comprehend more effectively when their unique, individual talents, abilities, and capacities are engaged.

When used and understood, these Brain/Mind Learning Principles challenge traditional views of learning and teaching. While direct instruction is important, functioning into a more complex approach to teaching is fundamental (Caine & Caine, 2011). In effect, scientists of the brain and mind have shown that even young, elementary learners really do make sense of their own experience and construct meanings for themselves and in association with others (Wolfe & Nevills, 2009).

THREE ELEMENTS THAT
BUILD THE BRIDGE TO TEACHING

After completing the twelve principles of brain/mind learning, we came to some powerful conclusions! We realized that regardless of how many strategies teachers used, those strategies needed to be integrated into a new view of how learning and teaching function in a brain-compatible (brain-based, brain-focused, etc.) school and classroom. Grasping the overall frame should come first. It seemed to us that there are three critical elements. Although they can be defined individually to some extent, each in fact is a part of and contributes to the other two.

1. Relaxed Alertness. The first element is "relaxed alertness," which is the optimal state of mind for the learner and the learning environment. It emerges in part from principle 11, which shows how sensitive human beings and consequently their brains are to threat and helplessness. Relaxed alertness also emerges, in part, from principle 3—demonstrating the necessity for intrinsic challenge and the search for personal meaning, personal choice, personal questions, and personal decision making. Other principles show that relationship and community are critical ingredients of relaxed alertness.

2. Orchestrated Immersion. The second element is the orchestrated immersion of the learner in complex experience in which content is embedded. This is a natural consequence of the view that every system of a person participates in learning, that the way to integrate all of the body/brain/mind systems and to have them functioning as a united whole is through experience, and that at the heart of learning is the need to solve personal problems posed by experience. That is why we define "learning" as "making sense of experience, and developing new capacities to act in and on the world."

3. Active Processing. The third element is the active processing of experience. This is essential because the key to learning from experience is to "mine" it for the insights that it has to offer—in other words, dig more deeply. This emerges from several sources. One is the innate drive to find meaning by looking for patterns. Another is the importance of elaboration in consolidating memory. An example of an approach that uses active processing is the Socratic method. Ultimately,

active processing involves a continuous interaction between learner and the teacher (in which nonjudgmental but challenging questioning, analysis, deep observation, and consolidation are all involved, referring regularly to standards and essential content and skills). Active processing is often ignored but is absolutely critical. It is a huge shift from "telling" and truly represents a new role for the teacher. Active processing includes standards and essential content and skills.

NEXT STEPS: THE INTERACTION OF PERCEPTION AND ACTION

Once we realized that the learning we envisioned was so dependent upon the dynamic engagement of the learner, it forced us to dig deeper into the research. A major breakthrough came with, among many references, neuroscientist Joaquin Fuster's book *Cortex and Mind* (2003). It became clear to us that every organism (and therefore every one of us) has to develop in two basic and interconnected ways that are indispensable aspects of survival and success—of the continuation of life itself. This is the dance of perception and action—a focus that has been emerging slowly from several different perspectives in recent times (Fuster, 2003; Maturana et al., 1998; Noe, 2004; Thompson, 2007). From a biological perspective, the human brain and body are designed to learn by seeking to make sense of what they are perceiving, by acting, and by dealing with the consequences. We do it every day, and it is as natural as breathing. Fuster (2003) made clear how the human cortex is developed on the basis of dealing with personally relevant questions or challenges that lead to action and feedback.

Where can we see this happening? When you see kids engrossed in video games, you are watching perception/action cycles in practice. It begins with curiosity and a desire to find out or accomplish more and leads to the need for more information, taking action to discover more by solving a problem and getting feedback, and then applying what has been learned to go further and deeper. The cycle is repeated many times and incorporates both a great deal of practice using particular tools and insights that have been acquired and the persistent drive to solve more problems and apply solutions that work for them.

Perception/action cycles play out continuously in ordinary, everyday experience. They recur over and over throughout life as people test, and either confirm or change, the ways in which they do things. In a general sense, therefore, this is the foundational organizer for natural learning. It underlies the making sense of experience and acquiring what we have called "performance knowledge" (Caine & Caine, 2001, 2011). Performance knowledge is a blend of the capacities to perceive and act appropriately in the real world.

We finally understood why the principles did not translate into today's classrooms. We recognized that from the very beginning we had always envisioned a much more learner-centered type of teaching. The brain is made for dynamic, interactive environments that challenge students to apply and engage with new ideas and experiences. The problem was the static approach to teaching dictated by the old meme. Most teachers spend too much time on their own plans for direct instruction and far too little on what kinds of questions drive motivation and enthusiasm. Once this changes, the principles and three elements make total sense and can easily be integrated into a model of learning that relies on experience.

MAKING IT PRACTICAL FOR EDUCATORS: THE GUIDED EXPERIENCE APPROACH

The frame now becomes clear.

- At the core of natural learning is the dance of perception and action. Learners make sense of experience by solving authentic problems and mastering new ways of taking action.
- The entire body, brain, and mind participate, as documented through the twelve principles. It is the whole system that perceives and reacts to a situation and makes sense of it. As a minimum, "making sense" is a process that engages emotions, social relationships, grasp of the physical context, physical action, state of mind, and individual predispositions and ways of interpreting life.
- Educators can guide this entire process by framing it in terms of the three elements we described above. They need to generate and maintain relaxed alertness as the state of mind in individuals and in the community at large; generate sufficiently complex experiences in which

content is embedded; and continuously guide students by providing ongoing feedback that focuses on high standards and essential skills. By working the three elements in this way, the underlying dance of perception and action is engaged and guided effectively.

This type of teaching is done by great teachers in many different settings and using different terminology. For instance, it is evident in good project-based learning, including what Apple Education calls "challenge learning." It can be found in the MetSchools (http://www.metschools. com/about.php). We have documented it in some detail in two amazing schools in Australia and Southern California (Caine & Caine, 2011). To the question of how well these students do on standardized tests, the answer is very well indeed. Almost all of the places implementing some version of perception/action learning have come at it in their own way. So they use creative and dynamic processes that automatically differentiate learning and that motivate and challenge students.

We call our own version the "Guided Experience Approach," and it is spelled out more formally below. We do this in part to ensure that the process is complete, because critical and essential steps are often left out. For instance, generating complex experience is all well and good, but most of the benefit is lost if the experience is not unpacked and processed in depth.

Guided Experience Approach

We present the Guided Experience Approach here in a linear form for the sake of convenience. Experienced teachers will know that it is nonlinear but that it is essential for all elements to be included.

- Begin with a multisensory immersive experience. This is a direct, real-world experience that constitutes a student's preliminary exposure to a new subject or material to be explored.
- Sensory processing of phenomena generated by the experience. This expands awareness of the details and previous experience, and triggers greater interest.
- Actor (student)-centered adaptive questions. These are based on authentic student interests and may emerge out of their own lives in some way.
- Planning, organizing, and doing research and skill development. This begins the real inquiry into the topic. It combines student research,

collective and individual inquiry, teacher-led sessions, explanations, and direct instruction on occasion. Skill development is incorporated, as students read, write, research, or pursue deeper understanding and do more processing.

- Creating a product shows what is known and takes the learning deeper. This culminates in the application of new skills and new understanding. Practical application both enhances accuracy and demonstrates what has been understood and mastered.
- Formative and summative assessments handled with ongoing active processing. Active processing is essential and nonnegotiable. Throughout the entire process of student-driven learning, the teacher, fellow students, and other experts continually challenge student thinking, expressed assumptions, mastery of concepts, and accuracy.
- Formal feedback. Final products are essential to this process. Public demonstrations, presentations, models, or documentations of all kinds take place. Attention is paid to issues ranging from the appropriate use of vocabulary to the ability to answer spontaneous questions raised by both experts and novices. So assessment is based on performance and one's ability to verbally explain and present what has been learned using appropriate vocabulary and definitions. Note that assessment does *not* need to be a grade.

The Guided Experience Approach calls for technology to be infused throughout. Technology can be used at every stage, ranging from conducting research, using communication tools and resources, and the creating and presenting of final unique and creative projects. Notice also the almost automatic inclusion of higher-order thinking, that is, executive functioning of the human brain fostered by this approach. Within the Guided Experience Approach, there is a need for constant decision making, planning, analyzing, negotiating, and reflecting—both individually and collectively (Caine & Caine, 2001).

FINAL COMMENT ON A NEW WORLD

A large-scale move to teaching based on natural learning requires many shifts in our collective beliefs about learning, teaching, and "schooling." It will require a fundamental shift in how everyone else sees his or her role and responsibilities. Ultimately, however, it makes more sense for those who will be living in a connected, information-driven world. Fortunately, this approach is very compatible with the new science standards still being finalized. It is also highly compatible with the California teaching standards on the incorporation of technology into the classroom. In fact, we contend that the shift to this approach is essential for a world increasingly dominated by information technology.

- Information is available from a vast range of resources at any time of day or night. The tools for accessing that information are already in the hands of students, and many schools are accelerating the process by, for instance, providing individual students with iPads and other mobile computing devices.
- While teacher expertise is important, expertise in almost all spheres of activity is also readily available elsewhere.
- Students can and do connect with each other and with others across cities, regions, and the world.

For these and other reasons, it is absolutely vital for educators to reconceive their roles and function as guides and facilitators, rather than as dispensers of information. The Guided Experience Approach provides a framework for rethinking the role of the teacher so that the learning capacities with which all students are naturally endowed can be more readily accessed.

REFERENCES

Begley, S. (2007). *Train your mind, change your brain: How a new science reveals our extraordinary potential to transform ourselves*. New York: Ballantine Books.

Bransford, J. D., Brown, A. L., & Cocking, R. R. (2000). *How people learn: Brain, mind, experience, and school*. Washington, DC: National Academy Press.

Caine, R. N., & Caine, G. (2011). *Natural for a connected world: Education, technology and the human brain*. New York: Teachers College Press.

Caine, G., & Caine, R. N. (2001). *The brain, education and the competitive edge.* Lanham, MD: Scarecrow Press.

Caine, R. N., & Caine, G. (1991, 1994). *Making connections: Teaching and the human brain.* Menlo Park, CA: Addison-Wesley.

Caine, R. N., Caine, G., McClintic, C. L., & Klimek, K. J. (2009). *Twelve brain/ mind learning principles in action: Developing executive functions of the human brain* (2nd ed.). Thousand Oaks, CA: Corwin.

Capra, F. (1996). *The web of life: A new scientific understanding of living systems.* New York: Anchor.

Combs, A. W. (1999). *Being and becoming: A field approach to psychology.* New York: Springer.

Conlan, R. (Ed.). (1999). *States of mind: New discoveries about how our brains make us who we are.* New York: Wiley.

Cozolino, L. (2013). *The social neuroscience of education: Optimizing attachment and learning in the classroom.* New York: Norton.

Damasio, A. R. (2005). *Descartes' error: Emotion, reason and the human brain.* New York: Avon Books.

Damasio, A. R. (1999). *The feeling of what happens: Body and emotion in the making of consciousness.* New York: Harcourt Brace.

Damasio, A. R. (1994). *Descartes' error: Emotion, reason and the human brain.* New York: Avon Books.

Deci, E. L., & Ryan, R. L. (2002). *The handbook of self-determination research.* New York: University of Rochester Press.

Deci, E. L., & Ryan, R. L. (1985). *Intrinsic motivation and self-determination in human behavior.* New York: Plenum Press.

Denkla, M. B. (1999). A theory and model of executive function: A neuropsychological perspective. In G. Lyon & N. Krasnegor (Eds.), *Attention, memory, and executive function* (pp. 263–278). Baltimore: Brookes.

Diamond, M. C., & Hobson, J. (1998). *Magic trees of the mind.* New York: Penguin Putnam.

Doige, N. (2007). *The brain that changes itself: Stories of personal triumph from the frontiers of brain science.* New York: Penguin Books.

Fuster, J. M. (2003). *Cortex and mind: Unifying cognition.* New York: Oxford University Press.

Gardner, H. (2006). *Multiple intelligences: New horizons* (rev. ed.). New York: Basic Books.

Gendlin, E. T. (1982). *Focusing.* New York: Bantam.

Gibbs, R. W. (2007). *Embodiment and cognitive science.* New York: Cambridge University Press.

Goldberg, E. (2001). *The executive brain: Frontal lobes and the civilized mind.* New York: Oxford University Press.

Goleman, D. (2006). *Social intelligence: The new science of human relationships.* New York: Bantam Books.

Gopnik, A., Meltzoff, A. N., & Kuhl, P. K. (1999). *The scientist in the crib: Minds, brains, and how children learn.* New York: William Morrow.

Hillman, J. (1996). *The soul's code: In search of character and calling.* New York: Warner Books.

Hurley, S. L. (2006). Bypassing conscious control: Unconscious imitation, media violence, and freedom of speech. In S. Pockett, W. P. Banks, & S. Gallagher (Eds.), *Does consciousness cause behavior? An investigation of the nature of volition* (pp. 301–338). Cambridge, MA: MIT Press.

Huttenlocher, P. R. (2002). *Neural plasticity; The effects of environment on the development of the cerebral cortex.* Perspectives in Cognitive Neuroscience. Cambridge, MA: Harvard University Press.

Iacoboni, M., Woods, R. P., Brass, M., Bekkering, H., Mazziotta, J. C., & Rizzolatti, G. (1999). Cortical mechanisms of human imitation. *Science, 286,* 2526–2528.

Lakoff, G., & Johnson, M. (1999). *Philosophy in the flesh: The embodied mind and its challenge to Western thought.* New York: Basic Books.

Lave, J., & Wenger, E. (1991). *Situated learning: Legitimate peripheral participation.* New York: Cambridge University Press.

Lazarus, R. S. (1999). *Stress and emotion: A new synthesis.* New York: Springer.

LeDoux, J. E. (1996). *The emotional brain.* New York: Simon & Schuster.

Maturana, H. R., Varela, F. J., & Paolucci, R. (1998). *The tree of knowledge: The biological roots of human understanding.* Boston, MA: Shambhala Publications.

Noe, A. (2004). *Action in perception.* Cambridge, MA: MIT Press.

O'Keefe, J., & Nadel, L. (1978). *The hippocampus as a cognitive map.* Oxford, UK: Clarendon Press.

Panksepp, J. (1998). *Affective neuroscience.* New York: Oxford University Press.

Pert, C. B. (1997). *Molecules of emotion.* New York: Scribner.

Pessoa, L. (2008, February). Opinion: On the relationship between emotion and cognition. *Nature Reviews Neuroscience, 9,* 148–158.

Peterson, C., Maier, S., & Seligman, M. (1995). *Learned helplessness: A theory for the age of personal control.* New York: Oxford University Press.

Restak, R. M. (2001). *The secret life of the brain.* Washington, DC: Joseph Henry Press.

Rizzolatti, G., & Sinigaglia, C. (2006). *Mirrors in the brain: How our minds share actions and emotions.* Oxford: Oxford University Press.

Robson, D. (2011, October 21). Your clever body: Thinking from head to toe. *New Scientist*. Retrieved from http://www.newscientist.com/article/mg21228341.500-your-clever-body-thinking-from-head-to-toe.html.

Sapolsky, R. (1998). *Why zebras don't get ulcers: An updated guide to stress, stress-related diseases, and coping*. New York: W. H. Freeman.

Schacter, D. (1996). *Searching for memory: The brain, the mind, and the past*. New York: Basic Books.

Shermer, M. (2008, November 25). Patternicity: Finding meaningful patterns in meaningless noise; Why the brain believes something is real when it is not. *Scientific American*. Retrieved from http://www.scientificamerican.com/article.cfm?id=patternicity-finding-meaningful-patterns&page=2.

Sternberg, R. J. (2008). *Cognitive psychology* (5th ed.). Belmont, CA: Wadsworth.

Sternberg, R. J., & Grigorenko, E. (2001). *Environmental effects on cognitive abilities*. Mahwah, NJ: Erlbaum.

Sylwester, R. (2012). Common core state standards; Part 2: Beginning the search for an appropriate education. *Information Age Education Newsletter, 101*. Retrieved from http://i-a-e.org/newsletters/IAE-Newsletter-2012-101.html.

Sylwester, R. (2007). *The adolescent brain: Reaching for autonomy*. Thousand Oaks, CA: Corwin.

Thompson, E. (2007). *Mind in life: Biology, phenomenology, and the science of mind*. Boston, MA: Belknap Press of Harvard University Press.

Varela, F. J., Thompson, E., & Rosch, E. (1991). *The embodied mind: Cognitive science and human experience*. Cambridge, MA: MIT Press.

Wiedenfeld, S. A., O'Leary, A., Bandura, A., Brown, S., Levine, S., & Raska, K. (1990). Impact of perceived self-efficacy in coping with stressors on components self-efficacy scales 21 of the immune system. *Journal of Personality and Social Psychology, 59*, 1082–1094.

Wolfe, P., & Nevills, P. (2009). Building the reading brain: PreK–3 (2nd ed.). Thousand Oaks, CA: Corwin.

Chapter Four

The Brain and Constructing Knowledge

Patrick M. Jenlink

Educational reform must start with how students learn and how teachers teach, not with legislated outcomes. After all, the construction of understanding is the core element in a highly complex process underpinned by what appears to be a simple proposition.

—J. G. Brooks and M. G. Brooks (2001)

The brain is a highly complex organ capable of receiving, perceiving, comprehending, storing, manipulating, controlling, and responding to a steady stream of data. As Renate Caine and Geoffrey Caine (1991) explained in their early work, "The brain's natural function is the search for meaning in experience. 'Brain-based learning' is confluent with the brain's natural rules for meaningful learning" (p. 88). The ability to link information from motor, sensory, and memory association areas is crucial for thought processing and the ability to contemplate and plan future actions, make decisions, and understand one's experiences in the world.

As a multimodal processor, the brain assembles patterns, makes meaning, sorts daily life and experiences, and then processes this information. In order for information to get to the hippocampus of the midbrain, which is where long-term memory is believed to be stored, the learner needs to use the information actively to strengthen new neural circuits. Memories are distributed throughout the cortex and are usually embedded in context. Eric Jensen (2000) is instructive on this point: "Our brain sorts and stores information based on whether it is heavily embedded in context or in content" (p. 222).

Today's educational system often expects students to retrieve content that has been removed from context. What we know about brain-based learning and constructivist teaching suggests alternatives that are more compatible with how learning occurs in the mind, as the mind of the learner is situated in the social contexts of the world. Michael Slavkin (2004), writing in *Authentic Learning: How Learning about the Brain Can Shape the Development of Students*, stated, "If brain-based pedagogy could be summed up in one sentence, it would be, Knowledge should be socially created" (p. 44).

In this chapter, I will explore the relationship between the brain and constructing knowledge, why constructing knowledge is critical for memory, and how a constructivist understanding of learning provides a pedagogical strategy for teachers implementing the science of brain-based learning.

THE BRAIN AS COGNITIVE ARCHITECTURE

How we, as educators, approach learning in consideration of designing learning activities determines, in large part, how students will learn and the successes, or failures, they will experience as learners. Our understanding of the brain is integral to our understanding of how learning takes place. Toward this goal, neuroscience and related brain-based research on cognitive load and learning suggest that we, as human beings, have what has been termed "cognitive architecture." According to Paul Kirschner (2002) and John Sweller (2004), human cognitive architecture determines the manner in which our cognitive, associative structures are organized. These associate structures are integral to how memory is stored.

Long-Term and Short-Term Memory

Memory, long term and short term, as a function of the brain's cognitive architecture, occurs as the brain undertakes complex, multipath neuronal growth. The organic nature of the brain is reflected in its ability to create memory and evolve the cognitive structures that enable us to learn. The processes of internalization and externalization that enable the individual to experience his or her cultural and social contexts, and to learn within those contexts, also enable the brain to create long-term and short-term memory (Kirschner, 2002).

Short-term or working memory is defined as the memory that is used for all conscious activities such as reading text, and it is the only memory that we can monitor (Kirschner, 2002; Sweller, 2004). As Joseph LeDoux (2002) explains, "Working memory is one of the brain's most sophisticated capacities and is involved in all aspects of thinking and problem-solving" (p. 175).

Short-term or working memory allows a space where data, ideas, and motivations can be held together and manipulated for a bit as the long-term memory system encodes information to other parts of the cortex. Thus, as a person juggles information, shifting back and forth from one object or thought to the next, working memory helps an individual stay focused and derive meaning as it integrates information from verbal and nonverbal specialized systems (the way something looks, sounds, and smells).

Long-term memory, in contrast, is defined as the repository that consists of a large and relatively permanent store of information, knowledge, and skills (Kirschner, 2002; Sweller, 2004). Most cognitive scientists believe that long-term memory can hold unlimited amounts of information including large, complex interactions and procedures.

Detecting Patterns

As the brain works to create long-term and short-term memory, it interprets patterns in the external world, patterns that are created through cognitive and social interactions with others and the environment or social contexts within which experience is situated. The brain relies on patterns in order to predict what lies ahead. Without patterns, nothing makes sense. There exists some sense of predictive power in order to navigate through an environment. Building these navigational aids forms the basis for ongoing activity in the brain.

Equally important, as the brain works to make sense of patterns, it is also creating new patterns associated with memory. And as the brain works to detect patterns and create memory, it also works to evolve the cognitive structures or mental models and schemas that are integral to the brain's organic neural architecture.

The brain is continuously making elaborate mental maps of how it perceives the world (Carter, 1999). As an individual experiences life, these mental maps are revised and updated. This is why early learning in life is so important for children because what is learned early on becomes the foundation for subsequent learning. As LeDoux (2002) explains, "Much of the self is learned by making new memories out of old ones. Just as learning is the process of creating memories, the memories created are dependent on things we've learned before" (p. 96). Thus, for learning and instruction, the most important feature of long-term memory (the permanent storehouse of knowledge and skills) is not its capacity but, more importantly, its networking efficiency for acquiring, processing, and storing general knowledge about objects, events, or situations.

Psychologists refer to these associative structures as mental models or schemas. When we learn something new, the information is not passively inscribed at the end of our memory tape; rather, it is integrated into a preexisting schema (Bruer, 1993). These associative structures influence the way we notice, interpret, and remember. Thus, effective instruction considers a student's prior experiences.

Brain-Based Learning Principles

It is the cognitive architecture of the human brain that enables learning. As an individual experiences various events and activities, he or she internalizes what is experienced, developing and evolving associate structures, mental models, or schemas. The principles of brain-based learning help us to understand how the brain learns and how knowledge is created and stored in memory (see Renate Caine and Geoffrey Caine's discussion in chapter 3 in this volume for more detail). These principals also help us to understand the need for pedagogical practices that serve as an interface for the cognitive architecture of the learner, the content or knowledge to be learned, and the context where learning is situated.

Context and content are enormously important. A single fact can be seen in many different contexts. One subject or issue is always related to many other subjects or issues. In this sense, there is an interconnectedness between multiple facts and multiple subjects, and within the subjects. A subject is understood if relationships with other areas are recognized. In this way, the subject or facts "make sense" and have meaning. What is called for, in this scenario, is curricula that embodies brain-based learning principles and at the same time pedagogical practices that embrace the cognitive and social nature of learning.

In the intersection of these two points, we must recognize that the brain processes information all the time. It naturally responds in a global way to the context of the environment in which it is immersed. As Renate Caine, Geoffrey Caine, Carol McClintic, and Karl Klimek (2005) have explained, the brain is a "parallel processor." Information is processed for many different functions at the same time. The interconnections between various parts of the brain make this possible. As the cognitive architect of learning experiences, the teacher must create an authentic world for the learner that recognizes the complexity of learning.

Acknowledging the cognitive architecture of the brain is important; principles of brain-based learning enable us to understand the nature of the brain. Equally important is an understanding of the pedagogical interface that exists between the learner and the teacher. The teacher becomes, in a sense, a cognitive architect responsible for designing and operationalizing a learning environment that is compatible with brain-based learning and at the same time understands the cognitive architecture of the learner. While traditional views of learning have followed behaviorism as a theory, more recent advancements in philosophy and theory of learning have focused on constructivism: cognitive and social constructivist views of learning.

A CONSTRUCTIVIST VIEW OF LEARNING

Understanding the relationship between the human brain and the construction of knowledge requires that we first examine basic precepts of learning. Learning is complex, and not all theories acknowledge this complexity in the same way. More traditional theories of learning, such as behaviorism, advocate for a transmission model of learning that is characterized as teacher centered (Bigge & Shermis, 1999; Tynjälä, 1999). These theories assume that knowledge exists extant in the world, ready to be delivered to the learner.

What we know about how the brain works, how its cognitive architecture functions, is that we experience the world, detect patterns, make sense of the patterns, and integrate our experiences and understanding of patterns as long-term and short-term memory. Constructivist views of learning align well with our understanding of the brain's cognitive architecture and the situated nature of our experiences in the world.

Constructivism is identified as a term for a set of epistemological theories that are grounded in a belief that meaning is constructed in the minds of individuals through the cognitive processing of interactions in the world. The constructivist paradigm of learning consists of two fields of philosophical thought on constructivism: cognitive constructivism and social constructivism.

Cognitive Constructivism

The cognitive view of constructivism, exemplified by Jean Piaget (1952, 1957), posits that people develop universal forms or structures of knowledge that enable them to experience reality. Knowledge is individually constructed and is based on the knower's intellectual development as she or he experiences reality during physical and social activity. In cognitive constructivism, the teacher's role as facilitator is to pose problems that challenge children's conceptions of reality.

Cognitive constructivism is important because it clearly locates learning in the mind of the individual and because it defines it as an active process of mental construction linked to interactions with the environment. This epistemological theory helps us to understand that knowledge is constructed in very different ways, by people in different stages of development; for example, novices to a field construct meaning differently than experts.

Cognitive constructivism also posits the interrelated process of assimilation and accommodation to enable mental construction (Rumelhart & Norman, 1981), and so links all new learning to learners' preexisting knowledge, bringing the issue of misconceptions and their nature more clearly in focus. Cognitive constructivism gives us the notion of knowledge organized internally as mental schemas that are in some broad sense peculiarly human.

Social Constructivism

The social view of constructivism, exemplified by Lev Vygotsky (1978, 1986), posits that knowledge is co-constructed through social and cultural contexts, rendering reality nonobjective. Knowledge socially constructed as reality is created during physical and social activity. The teacher's role is to be a collaborator who participates with the children in constructing reality by engaging in open-ended inquiry that elicits and addresses student (mis)conceptions.

Vygotsky (1978) maintained that, while taking place in individual minds, all learning results from social interaction and that meaning is socially constructed through communication, activity, and interactions with others. He believed that cognitive skills and patterns of thinking are not primarily determined by innate factors (as in genetic epistemology) but rather the products of the activities practiced in the social institutions of the culture in which the individual lives.

Vygotsky (1978) viewed the construction of meaning as a two-part, reciprocal process. According to Vygotsky, meanings are first enacted socially and then internalized individually; internal conceptualizations, in turn, guide social interactions. Vygotsky (1986) was particularly concerned with the role of language in thinking and learning. He believed that language and thought were intimately related. While at first a child seems to use language for superficial social interaction, at some point, he contended, this language is internalized to structure the child's thinking.

Another important concept in Vygotsky's (1978) learning theory is his notion of the zone of proximal development, the distance between the actual development level as determined by independent problem solving and the level of potential development as determined through problem solving under adult guidance or in collaboration with more capable peers. Vygotsky claimed that all learning occurs in this zone, which bridges the gap between what is known and what can be known, through adult/ instructor guidance or peer collaboration.

Social constructivism reminds us that learning is essentially a social activity, that meaning is constructed through communication, collaborative activity, and interactions with others. It highlights the role of social interactions in meaning making, especially the support of more knowledgeable others in knowledge construction.

Scaffolding, mediation of learning, and interaction with more experienced others is important to learning. Moreover, social constructivism encourages us to consider the critical function of language as the vehicle of thought and therefore of knowing and learning, and the ways in which knowledge and knowing are culturally and historically determined and realized.

Across the Epistemological Theories

John Bransford, Ann Brown, and Rodney Cocking (2000) noted that, according to constructivist theories, cognitivist and social, all learning involves mental construction, no matter how one is taught. All learning, it is argued, occurs in our minds as we create and adjust internal mental structures or schemas to accommodate our ever-growing and ever-changing stores of knowledge. Thus, according to constructivists, all learning is an active process and all knowledge is unique to the individual, whether acquired from lecture and text or discovered through experience. All learning, according to constructivists, is therefore intimately tied to experience and the contexts of experience, no matter how or where that learning takes place (Bransford, Brown, & Cocking, 2000).

A general set of constructivist learning principles have evolved from both cognitive and social constructivist theories that include the following: (1) learning is an active process; (2) learning is a social activity; (3) learning is contextual; (4) learning consists of both constructing meaning and constructing systems of meaning; (5) prior knowledge is needed for an individual to learn; (6) learning is dependent on mediational tools and artifacts; (7) learning is a process of internalization/externalization; (8) learning occurs in zones of proximal development; (9) learning is a longitudinal, adaptive, recursive process; (10) learning is both a conscious and an unconscious process; (11) the development of meaning is more important than the acquisition of a large set of concepts or skills; and (12) motivation is essential for learning (e.g., Brooks & Brooks, 2001; Brown, Collins, & Duguid, 1989; Bruner, 1966; Bruner & Garton, 1978; Fosnot, 1996; Leont'ev, 1978; Piaget, 1952, 1957, 2001; Phillips, 1985; Prawat, 1996; Resnick, 1985; Resnick & Collins, 1996; von Glasersfeld, 1989, 1995; Vygotsky, 1986).

THE BRAIN AND CONSTRUCTING KNOWLEDGE

Ernst von Glasersfeld's work (1986, 1987, 1989, 1995) in understanding constructivism as it applies to teaching and learning is particularly instructive in considering the process of constructing knowledge, as it sets forth several precepts that describe knowing and knowledge in their development, nature, function, and purpose. First, von Glasersfeld stated how knowledge is, and is not, made. Knowledge is constructed internally through cognitive reasoning; it is not passively received through the senses or by any form of communication. This first principal is significant to our understanding of brain-based learning and the advancement of cognitive architecture as the means by which the brain learns.

Second, von Glasersfeld described the importance of social interaction in the construction of knowledge. Social interactions between and among individuals, as learners, are central to the building of knowledge. Social interaction creates patterns and at the same time presents patterns in beliefs, concepts, and ideas derived from other individuals, and from which other individuals act and interact.

Third, the character of cognition is functional and adaptive. Cognition and the knowledge it produces are a higher form of adaptation in the biological context. This principle aligns well with our understanding of brain-based learning and the cognitive architecture that enables us to learn, construct knowledge, and create memories. The brain is an organ designed to learn.

Fourth, von Glasersfeld described what the purpose of cognition is and what it is not. Cognition's purpose is to serve the individual's organization of his or her experiential world; cognition's purpose is not the discovery of an objective ontological reality. Cognition enables us to internalize what we experience, detect patterns, and make sense of both experiences and patterns.

In examining the relationship between the brain, as cognitive architecture, and the construction of knowledge as understood from a constructivist perspective, there are three interrelated processes that work to construct knowledge. The first is internalization/externalization, which directs attention to how the brain detects patterns and assimilates and accommodates information (ideas, concepts, and experiences). The second is mediation, which occurs through the use of cognitive tools and cultural artifacts. And the third is the process of situating cognition.

Internalization/Externalization

John Dewey (1933), writing in *How We Think*, noted the relationship between internalization and externalization when he stated, "Every living creature, while it is awake, is in constant interaction with its surroundings. It is engaged in a process of give and take—of doing something to objects around it and receiving back something from them—impressions, stimuli. This process of interacting constitutes the framework of experience" (p. 36). We internalize, as learners, our external experiences, and in turn we externalize our understanding as we create new mediational tools and cultural artifacts. Dewey's framework of experience provides a foundation from which to build an understanding of how the brain constructs knowledge.

As the brain experiences the world, it internalizes the experience. In this sense, internalization implies that ideals or beliefs and concepts are internalized into our mental models or schemas. Our use of cultural artifacts such as language, books, and computers enables us to learn in new ways, and this learning is incorporated into our existing memory. Externalization implies that we create new artifacts. As our mental models or schemas are changed, we produce new artifacts introduced back in to the culture.

Internalization of external experiences is derived from social interactions that are mediated through the use of artifacts, and as such, internalization is simultaneously an individual and a social process. Relatedly, externalization is also an individual and a social process through which the application of schemas and cognitive processes work to create/transform existing semiotic, ideal/conceptual, and material artifacts, and animate learning.

Internalization is a process that occurs simultaneously in social practice and in the mind. The appropriation of semiotic artifacts—symbol systems—as an internalization process translates into the transformation of communicative language into inner speech. Through internalization processes, the individual constructs his or her mind in interaction with the external social world(s) of other individuals.

In this sense, learning is active, social, and situated in particular physical, social, and cognitive contexts. It involves the ongoing development of complex and interrelated mental structures or schemas, and the construction of knowledge is, to a greater or lesser degree, distributed across individuals, tools, and artifacts. When considering the act of teaching, constructivism shifts the pedagogical focus away from instruction in the more traditional sense and toward a pedagogical focus that is brain based and learner centered.

Central to constructivism, as a set of epistemological learning theories, is the notion that meaning is imposed on the world rather than extant in it. Constructivists believe that we impose meaning; that is, meaning is constructed in our minds as we interact with the physical, social, and mental worlds we inhabit. Further, constructivists believe that we make sense of our experiences by building and adjusting such internal knowledge structures or schemas that collect and organize our perceptions of and reflections on reality. Simply stated, we internalize our experiences as memories.

Constructivist learning theories, both cognitive and social, help us to understand and consider how, pedagogically, to assist the learner in transferring knowledge into true learning. There is a high level of compatibility between the principles of brain-based learning as discussed by Caine and Caine (see chapter 3 in this volume) and constructivist learning theories. Constructivists believe that students, as learners, need to make meaning from active participation in the learning process while building personal interpretations of the world based on experiences and interactions. Constructivist learning theories also promote the idea that learning is embedded in the context in which it is used and that authentic tasks should be performed in meaningful, realistic settings. Jeff Boulton (2002) is instructive on this point: "Constructivist learning theory is based on the assumption that learners construct knowledge as they attempt to make sense of their experiences. What we know depends on the kinds of experiences that we have had and how we organize these into existing knowledge structures" (p. 3). Existing knowledge structures can be compared to the existing neural network in the brain. Learning occurs as neural connections are developed. As these neural connections develop within the existing knowledge structures in the brain, the student constructs individual meaning from information and activities. Thus, brain-based learning follows the tenets of constructivist learning theory.

Mediation

A central principle of constructivist learning, as Michael Cole (1996) explains, is the use of artifact mediation: semiotic mediation through the use of different levels of artifacts. All human actions are mediated by the use of cultural artifacts; culture is defined as systems of shared meanings and as the social inheritance embodied in artifacts. Thus, culture mediates human interactions, shaping and in turn being shaped by the use of artifacts. Artifacts are, as Cole explains,

> an aspect of the material world that have been modified over the history of its incorporation into goal-directed action. By virtue of the changes wrought in the process of their creation and use, artifacts are simultaneously ideal (conceptual) and material. They are ideal in that their material form has been shaped by their participation in the interactions of which they were previously a part and which they mediate in the present. (p. 117)

Defined in this way, the distinction between the ideal and material properties of artifacts affirms both the inseparability of the material from the symbolic and the equal force of mediating human actions through the use of artifacts, whether one is considering language or a more concrete artifact such as a pencil.

Importantly, in constructivist learning, Cole (1996) identifies three levels of artifacts, including primary artifacts (words, writing instruments, telecommunication networks, mythical cultural personages, etc.); secondary artifacts (traditional beliefs, norms, constitutions, etc.); and tertiary artifacts (imagined worlds, creative representations, play, schemas, scripts, notions of context, etc.). These three levels of artifacts enable semiotic mediation of human action; most importantly, they animate learning with the cultural-historical nature of human interaction in educational settings.

Also of importance, memory as it relates to mediation and internalization/externalization processes can be differentiated into two different, distinct types: explicit memory and implicit memory. These are further broken down into categories that are more specific. Semantic and episodic memories are considered explicit memory, or memory that was learned by effort. Implicit memory is memory that is automatically learned. It deals with nonconscious (nonmental) cognitive processing of experiences.

Where the learner is engaged in internalization and externalization processes, he or she is also engaged in developing explicit and implicit memory, and evolving his or her mental models or schemas. As these processes occur, the learner's knowledge structures are evolving. Importantly, situating cognition, or immersion of the learner in learning experiences, enables the learner to make associations with other learning experiences. Constructivist pedagogy is attentive to creating authentic learning experiences that enable the construction of knowledge.

Situating Cognition

Situating cognition refers to learning within the context of practice; that is, the relationship between learners and the properties of specific contexts. Situating cognition reflects an understanding of knowledge as knowing about, which is a perceptual activity that always occurs within a context (Prawat & Floden, 1994). As John Brown, Allan Collins, and Paul Duguid (1989) explain, learning is always situated and progressively developed through situated activity. Learning involves more than acquiring a set of self-contained entities; it involves building a contextualized appreciation of these entities as artifacts, as well as for the situations through which these artifacts have value.

Mediating situated cognitive activities may be understood as a relationship between more experienced and less experienced individuals. In this relationship, more experienced others use conceptual as well as physical artifacts as tools for mediating cognitive reasoning and problem solving. Vygotsky's concept of zone of proximal development (ZPD) is instructive in understanding this relationship. He defined the ZPD as the distance between the actual development level of the learner and the level of potential development "determined through problem solving under . . . guidance or in collaboration with more capable peers" (Vygotsky, 1978). The zone is where mediated assistance, such as teaching or facilitating (through the resources of a more experienced other as cultural agent), and the individual (student or teacher as learner) development potential can interface.

Extending the concept of ZPD into human activity systems, Yrjo Engeström explained mediation as "the distance between the present everyday actions of the individuals and the historically new form of the societal activity that can be generated as a solution" (Engeström, 1987, p. 174). Mediation, then, represents the use of cultural artifacts (ideal and material) to assist less experienced individuals, less cognitively and consciously aware individuals, to learn in situ, as situated cognitive development within communities of practice.

It is important to note that situating cognition is compatible with the brain's nature functioning. As cognition is situated in contexts of experience and is supported in social and life experiences, the brain processes information. It naturally responds, reflexively, to the context of the learning environment in which it is immersed. Situating cognition also relies upon short-term and long-term memory in constructing knowledge.

Summary

Jerome Bruner (1971), writing in *Relevance of Education*, asks a profound and critically important question that goes to the heart of bridging between the epistemological nature of constructivism and brain-based learning: "Is there some sense in which principles of pedagogy can be derived from our knowledge of man as a species—from knowledge of his characteristic growth and dependence, of the properties of his nervous system, of his modes of dealing with culture?" (p. 118). A simple response might argue, rightly so, that the epistemological divide between constructivist and brain-based learning principles is not that wide. Both view learning as an active process in which learners construct their own understanding and knowledge of the world through action and reflection. Constructivists, much like advocates of brain-based learning, argue that individuals generate rules and mental models as the result of their experiences with both other human subjects and their environments and in turn use these rules and models to make sense of new experiences.

The brain as cognitive architecture is dependent on internalization/externalization, mediation, and situating cognition processes as interface between the associate, cognitive structures of the organic architecture and the social cognitive experiences of the learner's world. These three processes are integral to the pedagogical interface between the cognitive architecture of the brain and the teacher as cognitive architect responsible for creating experiences that assist students in making meaningful connections, making decisions, applying what has been learned, reflecting on their own thinking and accomplishments, and using critical thinking and feedback from others. Providing a rich, multisensory environment that embraces the multimodal nature of the brain through arts, music, storytelling, drama, emotions, and real-world context engages students' interests and fosters well-developed cognitive reasoning; it enables natural learning of the brain.

The relationship between the brain and constructing knowledge is explained, in large part, by understanding that constructivist epistemologies of learning, much like brain-based learning theories, acknowledge that all meaningful learning is complex and nonlinear; it is both cognitive and social, situated in its complexity. This means that teachers must use all available resources, including social-cultural resources of the community, to orchestrate dynamic learning environments. Teachers must overcome the natural preference for conveying information tied to clear directions and opportunities for students to "do it right" rather than to explore and experiment—in an active, constructivist, and brain-compatible way.

REFERENCES

Bigge, M. L., & Shermis, S. S. (1999). *Learning theories for teachers* (6th ed.). New York: Longman.

Boulton, J. (2002, February 26). Web-based distance education: Pedagogy, epistemology, and instructional design. Retrieved September 22, 2011, from http://www.usask.ca/education/coursework/802papers/boulton/boulton.pdf.

Bower, J., & Parsons, L. (2003). Rethinking the "lesser brain." *Scientific American, 289*, 50–57.

Bransford, J. D., Brown, A. L., & Cocking, R. (2000). *How people learn: Brain, mind, experience, and school*. Washington, DC: National Academy Press.

Brooks, J. G., & Brooks, M. G. (2001). *In search of understanding: The case for constructivist classrooms*. Upper Saddle River, NJ: Prentice Hall.

Brown, J. S., Collins, A., & Duguid, P. (1989). Situated cognition and the culture of learning. *Educational Researcher, 18*, 32–42.

Bruer, J. T. (1997, November). Education and the brain: A bridge too far. *Educational Researcher, 26*, 4–16.

Bruer, J. T. (1993). *Schools for thought: A science of learning in the classroom*. Cambridge, MA: MIT Press.

Bruner, J. S. (1971). *Relevance of education*. New York: Norton.

Bruner, J. S. (1966). *Toward a theory of instruction*. Cambridge, MA: Belknap Press of Harvard University.

Bruner, J. S., & Garton, A. (1978). *Human growth and development*. Oxford, UK: Clarendon Press.

Caine, R. N., & Caine, G. (1991). *Making connections: Teaching and the human brain*. Alexandria, VA: Association for Supervision and Curriculum Development.

Caine, R. N., Caine, G., McClintic, C., & Klimek, K. (2005). *Twelve brain/mind learning principles in action: The field book for making connections, teaching and the human brain*. Thousand Oaks, CA: Corwin.

Carter, R. (1999). *Mapping the mind*. Los Angeles: University of California Press.

Cole, M. (1996). *Cultural psychology: A once and future discipline*. Cambridge, MA: Harvard University Press.

Dewey, J. (1933). *How we think*. Lexington, MA: D.C. Heath.

Engeström, Y. (1987). *Learning by expanding: An activity-theoretical approach to development research*. Helsinki, Finland: Orienta-Konsultit.

Fosnot, C. T. (1996). *Constructivism: Theory, perspectives, and practice*. New York: Teachers College Press.

Jensen, E. (2000). *Brain-based learning*. San Diego: Brain Store.

Kirschner, P. A. (2002). Cognitive load theory: Implications of cognitive load theory on the design of learning. *Learning and Instruction, 12*, 1–10.

LeDoux, J. (2002). *Synaptic self: How our brains become who we are*. New York: Penguin.

Leont'ev, A. N. (1978). *Activity, consciousness, personality*. Englewood Cliffs, NJ: Prentice Hall.

Phillips, D. C. (1985). The good, the bad, and the ugly: The many faces of constructivism. *Educational Researcher, 24*(7), 5–12.

Phillips, D. (Ed.). (2000). *Constructivism in education: Opinions and second opinions on controversial issues*. Chicago: National Study for the Study of Education.

Piaget, J. (2001). *The psychology of intelligence* (2nd ed.). London: Routledge (originally published in 1950).

Piaget, J. (1957). *Construction of reality in the child*. London: Routledge.

Piaget, J. (1952). *The origins of intelligence in children*. New York: International Universities Press.

Prawat, R. S. (1996). Constructivisms, modern and postmodern. *Educational Psychology, 31*(3/4), 215–225.

Prawat, R. S., & Floden, R. E. (1994). Philosophical perspectives on constructivist views of learning. *Educational Psychology, 29*(1), 37–48.

Resnick, L. B. (1985). *Comprehending and learning: Implications for a cognitive theory of instruction*. Pittsburg: Learning Research and Development Center University of Pittsburg.

Resnick, L. B., & Collins, A. (1996). Cognition and learning. In T. Plomp & D. Ely (Eds.), *The international encyclopedia of educational technology* (2nd ed.; pp. 48–54). Oxford, UK: Pergamon Press.

Rumelhart, D. E., & Norman, D. A. (1981). Analogical processes in learning. In J. R. Anderson (Ed.), *Cognitive skills and their acquisition* (pp. 335–359). Hillsdale, NJ: Erlbaum.

Slavkin, M. (2004). *Authentic learning: How learning about the brain can shape the development of students*. Lanham, MD: Scarecrow Education.

Smilkstein, R. (2003). *We're born to learn: Using the brain's natural learning process to create today's curriculum*. Thousand Oaks, CA: Corwin.

Sweller, J. (2004). Instructional design consequences of an analogy between evolution by natural selection and human cognitive architecture. *Instructional Science, 32*, 9–31.

Tynjälä, P. (1999). Towards expert knowledge? A comparison between constructivist and a traditional learning environment in the university. *International Journal of Educational Research*, 31, 367–442.

von Glasersfeld, E. (1995). A constructivist approach to teaching. In L. Steffe & J. Gale (Eds.), *Constructivism in education* (pp. 3–16). Hillsdale, NJ: Lawrence Erlbaum.

von Glasersfeld, E. (1989). Constructivism in education. In T. Husen & N. Postlewaite (Eds.), *International encyclopedia of education* (Suppl.); (pp.162–163). Oxford, UK: Pergamon Press.

von Glasersfeld, E. (1987). Learning as a constructive activity. In C. Janvier (Ed.), *Problems of representation in the teaching and learning of mathematics* (pp. 3–17). Hillsdale, NJ: Lawrence Erlbaum.

von Glasersfeld, E. (1986). Steps in the construction of others and reality. In R. Trappl (Ed.), *Power, autonomy, and utopias: New approaches toward complex systems* (pp. 107–116). London: Plenum Press.

Vygotsky, L. S. (1986). *Thought and language* (Translation newly revised and edited by Alex Kozulin). Cambridge, MA: MIT Press.

Vygotsky, L. S. (1978). *Mind in society*. Cambridge, MA: Harvard University Press.

Part II

INSPIRATION

Case Studies of Success

In the second part of the book, the leaders are inspired by two very different case studies of successful implementation of brain-compatible and natural learning in schools. The first case is an elementary implementation that is taking place in a large suburban school district. Specifically, an early childhood school was developed in the Montessori Method but with the insights of current brain research. Although the field of neuroscience was not well advanced when Maria Montessori lived, largely due to the limitation of technology, many of her insights as a medical doctor would later be grounded in what has now been documented about the brain in both neuroscience and education.

The second inspiring case presented is a secondary-level, district-wide project in a large urban school district. A district mathematics director decided to use brain-compatible learning as a means of improving Algebra I performance and closing the gaps among ethnic groups. This courageous leader tells a heartfelt story of the journey to lead the algebra teachers of several dozen high schools into the world of natural and brain-compatible learning. In it she recounts the district's struggles but ultimate success.

At the conclusion of part II, "Inspiration," the following beliefs and paradigms should be apparent:

- We believe that brain-compatible learning works for all students in both elementary and secondary schools.
- We believe that brain-compatible learning will take many forms and approaches in schools as opposed to a one-size-fits-all model.

- We believe that brain-compatible learning programs can be successfully developed and implemented in today's educational climate and high-stakes testing environment.
- We believe that true innovative improvement for schools requires strong, deliberate, and ongoing leadership to be successful and that leadership can come in many forms or positions within an organization.

Chapter Five

Montessori Bilingual Education and Brain-Compatible Learning

Beverly J. Irby, Rafael Lara-Alecio,
Fuhui Tong, and Linda Rodriguez

Educators are in the only profession in which their job is to change the human brain every day.

—David Sousa (2011)

Maria Montessori began her work with children and curriculum development in the late nineteenth century. Being a medical doctor, she became affiliated with a psychiatric clinic, and it was there that she became interested in how children learn. In particular, she observed children who were mentally challenged. She saw such children responding positively to food that was thrown at them in an institutionalized, cold, nonstimulating environment. From that observation, she concluded the interest the children showed in the food was not related all together to the food as nourishment; rather, she concluded that they were responding to the food as a stimulant (Kramer, 1976; Standing, 1957).

From that incident in 1897, she initiated the development of stimulus educational materials for this group of children, and ultimately, she created what she called Sensorial Materials (Montessori, 1967). We believe that was likely Montessori's first encounter with a brain-based, neurological observation, which led to the beginning of the Montessori Method. Though she was not thinking about (nor was there advanced knowledge on the subject at that time) neurological brain activity or brain-based learning, Montessori intuitively developed a method of teaching and learning that may be recognized today some one-hundred-plus years later as one of the best programs of study for young children that is related to brain-based learning. She had written *Pedagogical Anthropology* in 1913 and reported on the then most current cranial studies. At that time, it seemed the science was to study the furrows, fissures, weight, and observational differences in human brains and animals; weight and other measurable differences between male and female brains and infants to adults; and observable abnormalities in brains. She included a drawing of the brain in the text that was remarkably accurate given the limited technology and infancy of the field of neurology. Even so, these were certainly some of the most up-to-date technological advances in brain research, but the world of neuroscience research clearly had not advanced sufficiently to understand actual brain activity and function in relation to the abovementioned observations of the early twentieth century.

Montessori moved forward with her research in the most logical manner in studying cognition related to teaching and learning and did so through the observation of children. Though she did not have modern tools at hand, she could almost be considered to have extrasensory perception or some type of divining ability in terms of how she developed the Montessori Method of teaching in her day as it relates today to the engagement of children with modern neuroscientific research–based and brain-based learning. We contend that the Montessori Method for young children, particularly for those who are English-language learners (ELL), is supported by the tenets of brain-based principles. In this chapter, we will review Montessori, bilingual, prekindergarten education incorporating the related tenets of brain-based learning for young children and data for the case of a public prekindergarten, Montessori, bilingual education program.

MONTESSORI EDUCATION TENETS AND BRAIN-BASED LEARNING FOR YOUNG CHILDREN

One of the basic principles behind the Montessori Method is "the fundamental difference between the child and the adult" and that "the child was a continual state of growth and metamorphosis, whereas the adult had reached the norm of the species" (Standing, 1957, p. 87). Montessori, again, quite ahead of her time, seemed to have arrived at this concept through her observations, and she reflected on this in her book *The Absorbent Mind* (Montessori, 1949; reprinted in 1989). According to Polk Lillard and Lynn Jessen (2003), new findings from research correspond with the discovery that the foundation of neural structures in the frontal lobes of the human brain is not fully developed until approximately age twenty-four. They indicated that the brain continually develops, and for individuals to achieve their full potential there must be interaction with their environment, and there must be input with sensorial awareness. Children's growth and metamorphosis can be observed through their increasing independence, coordinated gross and fine motor skills, language, and advancing will.

Renate Caine and Geoffrey Caine also have supported the notion of the developing brain. This particular concept related to Montessori education is born out in Caine and Caine's (1997) eleventh principle of their twelve Brain/Mind Learning Principles; the eleventh principle is complex learning that is enhanced by challenge and inhibited by threat. In fact, as one reads Montessori, one finds the brain-based optimized conditions for learning as proposed by Caine and Caine (2011): (a) relaxed alertness, which consists of low threat and high challenge; (b) orchestrated immersion, which places the learner in multiple, complex, authentic experiences; and (c) active processing, which is consistent experiential learning that is the basis for making meaning.

Epochs of Development

Four stages or epochs of mental metamorphosis or mental development were noted by Montessori. The first is during ages zero to six, and this epoch will be discussed in relation to the focus of this chapter. In the second epoch of development (ages six to twelve), Montessori identified a herd instinct in children (Standing, 1957). While she believed the first epoch to be devoted to the construction of the human individual, it is in the second epoch that children develop a group instinct. Montessori indicated that the second stage of childhood is marked by the strengthening of the reasoning faculty. On the moral plane, for instance, it examines the rightness and wrongness of actions (Standing, 1957). Montessori called the third epoch of development "adolescence" (ages twelve to eighteen). She subdivides this period into two stages: puberty (twelve to fifteen) and adolescence (fifteen to eighteen). The fourth epoch of development that Montessori identified is ages eighteen to twenty-four. During this epoch, there is a full time for the acquisition of knowledge. This stage, known as the time of the specialist mind, is when young adults are able to study their interests.

Returning now to the first epoch, which is the age range with which this case is concerned, Montessori defined the first stage of development (ages zero to six) to be the epoch of the absorbent mind, which subdivides in two stages: unconscious (ages zero to three) and conscious (ages three to six). In the first stage, children absorb the world through their unconscious intelligence. In the second stage, children take in consciously from the environment, using their hands, which become the instruments of the brain (Standing, 1957). Bringing Montessori into the twenty-first century with this stage, Sarah Hileman (2006) discusses brain-based research practices that encourage students to be actively engaged via experiential learning.

Montessori believed that it is this stage in which children learn more than in any other time period. In terms of brain development, according to John Bruer (1997), there are three well-established findings in developmental neurobiology: (1) starting at infancy and continuing into later childhood, there is a dramatic increase in the number of synapses that connect neurons in the brain; (2) there are experience-dependent critical periods in the development of sensory and motor systems; and (3)—in rats at least—complex, or enriched, environments cause new synapses to form. Thus, the brain knows how to developmentally scaffold itself. For example, in Broca's area, the region in the brain for language production, it has been determined that when this becomes myelinated, children develop speech and grammar. In Wernicke's area, the center of language comprehension, myelination occurs a good six months before Broca's area even starts. This is very clever, since individuals need to be able to understand language before they can produce it.

Starting in early infancy, there is a rapid increase in the number of synapses or neural connections in children's brains. Up to age ten, children's brains contain more synapses than at any other time their lives. Early childhood experiences fine tune the brain's synaptic connections (Bruer, 1997, p. 4). According to Usha Goswami (2009),

Learning is distributed across large networks of neurons, and so factors like the number of relevant neurons firing, their firing rates, the coherence of the firing patterns, and how "clean" they are for signalling the appropriate information will all vary depending on how the current environmental input activates the existing network (see Munakata, 2001). As the fibre connections growing in response to received inputs are strengthened over time, it can also become difficult to reorganise the system when a new learn-ing environment is experienced. This offers one potential mechanism for explaining why it is more difficult to learn a second language later in life (Munakata and McClelland, 2003). (Kindle location 556)

The more children are exposed to a rich environment in which they can practice language and engage in language, the greater the number of synaptic connections. Sousa (2010a) stated, "We are not born with mono-lingual, bilingual, or multilingual brains. Rather, the bilingual 'signature' that appears is most likely the result of environmental exposure to several languages during the child's early years." Furthermore, he noted,

> Another feature of structural differences in the brains of monolinguals and bilinguals is the thick cable of nerves that connects the two hemispheres—the corpus callosum—that was discussed earlier. It seems to be larger and more densely populated with neurons in bilinguals than in monolinguals, most likely to accommodate the multilanguage capacity (Coggins, Ken-nedy, & Armstrong, 2004). The implication here is that exposing very young children to other languages helps build the neural networks that will consolidate and process them. Furthermore, it seems that these networks will make it easier for these individuals to learn a third language later in life (Bloch et al., 2009). (Sousa, 2010a, Kindle location 864–869)

Though Montessori did not have the benefit of modern neuroscience, it seems that she was correct in her assumptions of early learning in chil-dren, because, according to Bruer (1997), the time of high synaptic den-sity and experiential fine tuning is a critical period in a child's cognitive development—and it is in Montessori's first epoch that she proposed that the brain could efficiently acquire and learn a wide range of skills.

Sensitive Periods in Development

The term "sensitive periods" was discovered by the Dutch scholar Hugo De Vries, who in 1900 confirmed the Mendelian laws of hered-ity (Kramer, 1988). Struck by the parallels between Montessori's theory and his own botanical, biological theories of the development of plants, De Vries (as cited in Kramer, 1988) suggested that Montessori make use of this term to describe her observations about the stages of children's growth and learning (Kramer, 1988). She did use the term and suggested these were windows of opportunity for children to learn about their world.

Edwin Standing (1957) noted that "during the development of certain organisms there come periods of special sensibility. These [transitory] periods of sensibility are related to certain elements in the environment toward which the organism was directed with an irresistible impulse and a well-defined activity" (p. 100). The intense and prolonged activity aroused and sustained by a sensitive period causes not fatigue but rather the reverse. In each sensitive period, the children are endowed with special powers, which help them to construct their personality through the acquisition of some well-defined characteristic or function (Montessori, 1914).

The sensitive period of two to four years of age is of great practical significance to administrators in their consideration of the development of a Montessori program. According to Standing (1957), children get a sense of the position of everything in the classroom very quickly just because of this sensitive period of order. In the Montessori program, this sensitive period is acknowledged by providing children with learning environments where everything had its proper place and must be kept. The environment is related to the neural development of the child. For example, Goswami (2009) indicated from a negative aspect that it is important to avoid creating learning environments that support the acquisition of maladaptive connections; that is, environments that feel unsafe or stressful (Kindle location 569). Furthermore, noting the importance of environment on brain development, Eric Jensen (2008) indicated that

> threatening environments can trigger chemical imbalances. Especially worrisome is the reduced level of serotonin, which is a strong modulator of emotions and subsequent behaviors; when serotonin levels fall, violence often rises. Threats also elevate levels of vasopressin, which has been linked to aggression. These imbalances can trigger impulsive and aggressive behavior that some researchers believe can lead to a lifetime of violence. (Kindle location 631–633)

Montessori, in 1917, recognized the importance of intelligence and relationship of the environment. Montessori was already forming her schema for her teaching and learning method when she asked, "What is intelligence?" and to which she replied, "Without rising to the heights of the definitions given by the philosophers, we may, for the moment, consider the sum of those reflex and associative or reproductive activities which enable the mind to construct itself, putting it into relation with the environment" (Montessori, 1917, Kindle location 2740–2742).

One of the earliest sensitive periods in the child's development is the one concerned with the acquisition of spoken language. Transitory as are all sensitive periods, once gone, it never returns (Standing, 1957). Shannon Helfrich (2011) indicates that "children's brains between birth and age six years are completely open to learning and integrating into their lives any language they are exposed to. During this sensitive period for language, a child can easily become bilingual (or more) and speak the language(s) without an accent" (p. 22).

According to Alice Renton (1998), in terms of language, Montessori averred that children unconsciously learn about the language itself and how it operates. Renton contended, rather, it is the exposure that children have to one or more languages that determines whether their linguistic potential will be developed. Renton stated that in the cases of some children, the natural linguist may be awakened by their family context, where the child might grow up with two or more languages being spoken at home (typically, this would not be occurring in low socioeconomic conditions of many of the recent Spanish-speaking immigrants who come to the United States). In the case of the children whom we will be introducing later in this chapter, their potential was influenced deeply at the Montessori pre-kindergarten school, where their native language was used to introduce a second, dominant language. As a component of Montessori in the case we present, the native language is practiced, advanced, and respected.

To Renton (1998), the home and the language of culturally and linguistically diverse learners should be not only respected but also maintained and developed as fully as possible. For these children, the mastery of the dominant language was also of vital importance. Culturally and linguistically diverse children should consider themselves functional in two cultures and in two languages. With the belief that primary language skills in a first language was the base for developing skills in a second language, Renton (1998) presented five basic principles of current second-language acquisition approaches that she suggested can be successfully implemented in a Montessori environment. Though the Montessori environment is rich, it is also organized. Organization is a principle that Montessori promoted for children. Caine and Caine (1994) indicated that based on the brain research of John O'Keefe and Lynn Nadel (1978), which suggested that the brain "automatically registers the familiar while simultaneously searching for and responding to novel stimuli" (p. 89), the "learning environment needs to provide stability and familiarity . . . routine classroom behaviors and procedures. At the same time, provision must be made to satisfy our curiosity and hunger for novelty, discovery, and challenge" (p. 89)—all components of the Montessori environment, and all components that support second-language acquisition.

First, Renton (1998) stated that second-language acquisition happens most naturally when the process closely resembles first-language acquisition. Renton adhered to the notion that effective second-language acquisition takes place when children are exposed to natural interactions and when the goal is communicative competence (Krashen, 1988).

Second, the environment that should promote second-language acquisition must provide comprehensible input (Krashen, 1988) and a supportive affective climate. This principle means that language should be understandable and meaningful. Undoubtedly, the concept of context plays a critical role in making language understandable and meaningful. According to Renton (1998), the concrete materials used in the Montessori Method have proved attractive to children, while at the same time they "embody specific concepts, and invite exploration through movement and the senses" (p. 31). Concrete materials and context is important for comprehensible input for language development. For example, according to Judy Willis (2010),

When we gain information by touching something, that sensation is recognized, and the memory ultimately stored in the parietal lobes at the top of the brain. However, when subjects were blindfolded for a week and received intense tactile-sensory Braille practice, their occipital visual cortex, which before the experiment did not respond to tactile stimuli, demonstrated new neural-circuit plasticity and fMRI activity. Their visual cortex became similar to those found in people blind from birth (Merabet et al., 2008). (Kindle location 1034–1038)

Third, second-language acquisition should foster a basic communicative proficiency and a cognitive academic proficiency. In a Montessori learning environment, both levels of language are continually being constructed and practiced (Renton, 1998). Social conversations among the learners and the teacher and lessons that target concept development are combined in the instruction of children. According to Lillard (2008), the Montessori curriculum promotes language and concept development. For example, she stated, "Montessori uses a wealth of materials for vocabulary development. In addition to simply labeling more common objects and actions as they learn to read and write, Montessori children learn the parts of the plant, the countries of the world, the variety of geological formations, and so on, even before age 6" (p. 333). Movement and object manipulation is also integrated into learning new vocabulary in the Montessori classroom; movement and tactile, kinesthetic activities are related to how the brain learns. Lillard stated that brain research supports purposeful movement in learning, as opposed to simply random movement. Montessori incorporates purposeful movement in learning via manipulation of materials in learning new vocabulary or in learning to read and write.

Fourth, second-language acquisition requires time. The three-year cycle proposed by Montessori programs provides time for children to move through various levels of second-language development. It was once assumed, in terms of brain research, that children would become confused if exposed to two languages (Redlinger & Park, 1980; Vihman, 1985). According to Lann Petitto and colleagues (2001), this was believed because one area in the brain had to be used primarily for processing the first language, and consequently, there would be little neural resources left for processing the second language. However, more recently, Diane Williams (2010) stated, "The results of neuroimaging research indicate that, rather than causing confusion in the brain, the brain adaptively uses language areas to process both languages efficiently" (Kindle location 1756–1757).

Finally, the fifth principle presented by Renton (1998) stated that languages are inseparable from culture, and the former are always learned most effectively in a cultural context. Indeed, as Renton indicated, "Culture shapes the child's first experiences, from which language arises" (Renton, 1998, p. 31). According to Mary Rothbart and colleagues (2009), researchers have found an influence of culture related to classroom training on brain neural network attention function and development.

Education of the Senses

Montessori identified a sensitive period for refinement of the senses. She thought there was a period (two and a half to six years of age) when the child refined senses and impressions of all kinds, in color, sound, shape, and texture. Goswami (2009) stated that based on neurological research, "if children are taught new information using a variety of their senses, learning will be stronger (that is, learning will be represented across a greater network of neurons connecting a greater number of different neural structures, and accessible via a greater number of modalities)" (Kindle location 583–584).

Montessori believed in the education of the senses, which aimed at "the refinement of the differential perception of stimuli by means of repeated exercises" (Montessori, 1964, p. 173). This was the period where Montessori gave the children sensorial materials, as shown in figure 5.1, that she had designed to stimulate and refine the senses (Standing, 1957). Alexander Rippa (1997) noted that Montessori thought sensory education was the basis of her method. To Montessori, it was necessary to begin the education of the senses in the formative period. To translate her ideas into practice, Montessori invented some ingenious and varied educational games (Rippa, 1997). The didactic apparatus for these games consisted of twenty-six separate items (cylinders, geometric insects, rectangular

Figure 5.1.   Children using sensorial material. Irby photo used with permission.

blocks, and colored tablets). Each piece of material was carefully graded and self-corrective. In addition, she designed and had manufactured lightweight, movable furniture; small chairs and tables replaced the then customary large, stationary desks. She also planned special activities to develop auditory skills (the "game of silence") and to encourage vocabulary enrichment and the use of correct and fluent speech (Rippa, 1997).

Neuroscientists have noted that environmental influences probably play a significant role in brain development (Rao et al., 2010; Shaw et al., 2006); therefore, it seems once again that Montessori was on target in developing an enriching and prepared environment for children to learn and express themselves freely (Montessori, 1912, reprinted 1997).

Another period identified by Montessori was the sensitive period related to social and emotional growth: learning good manners (also two and a half to six years of age). This period was perfect for learning good manners, such as opening and closing a door appropriately, safely handing a sharp instrument to another person, eating correctly, saluting, or being excused. Standing (1957) noted that according to Montessori, "When the education of children was organized in relation to their sensitive periods, they work with a sustained enthusiasm which had to be seen in order to be believed" (Standing, 1957, p. 133). This particular sensitive period for Montessori was one way in which she incorporated social and emotional input into the educational environment. According to Mary Helen Immordino-Yang and Matthias (2010), recent neuroscientific research includes the "interrelatedness of emotions and cognition and the importance of emotion in rational thought (Greene, Sommerville, Nystrom, Darley, & Cohen, 2001; Haidt, 2001; Immordino-Yang, 2008). Yet much of contemporary educational practice considers emotion as ancillary or even as interfering with learning" (Kindle location 1434–1437).

However, Montessori considered it essential to the learning process. In practice, it was determined by Angeline Lillard and Nicole Else-Quest (2006) in a quasi-experimental study that children who participated in a Montessori program were significantly more likely to be socially adept in resolving interpersonal problems and social negotiations. Furthermore, Goswami (2009) suggested that "biological, sensory and neurological influences on learning must become equal partners with social, emotional and cultural influences if we are to have a truly effective discipline of education" (Kindle location 702–703).

Emotional Development and Language Development

Michael Rosanova (1998) indicated that children's emotional development correlates with language development. Bearing this principle in
mind, Rosanova identified four developmental stages of a Montessori
community; namely, the preproduction, the early production, the speech
emergence, and the intermediate fluency stages. In their first year of the
program, children would only say isolated words, phrases, and routine
expressions, or would not speak in the target language at all. According
to Rosanova (1998), the children's first task was to develop social and
cognitive strategies that enabled them to understand and eventually to develop a receptive vocabulary. However, until this happens, children "get
distracted easily, often would not follow directions . . . and rely heavily on
contextual cues for understanding" (Rosanova, 1998, p. 37). The teacher's
role at this point was to provide a lot of demonstration and repetition, even
more than in a monolingual Montessori setting.

In the early production stage, many children have begun to produce
a variety of simple words and short phrases in the target language, and
they are also able to respond with one-word answers to questions. Contextual cues continue to be critical to children's understanding. Also,
the children's community gets stronger with children helping their peers
interpret and understand. As Rosanova (1998) suggested, the emergence
of interpretation among the children was critical for classroom behavior.

In the speech emergence stage, coherent dialogues begin to emerge.
Some children begin to speak the target language in longer phrases and
more fluently. A few of them, however, still struggle with the pronuncia-
tion or grammar. Despite these differences, most of the children are able
to get the message across.

Finally, in the intermediate fluency stage, the children who become more
capable of structuring cooperative work usually create roles for at least
some of the younger children. Younger children are exposed to episodes
of full sentences and connected narrative, which are provided by models
different from the teacher. This way, children become the models for their
younger peers, which is a concept promoted in Montessori education.

Rosanova (1998) concluded with a few recommendations for language-
immersion programs. First, survival vocabulary goals need to be established. It was important that children be exposed to richer vocabulary
than the traditional noun lists. Further, children who attain their goals

also need to be identified. Second, repetition of key grammatical forms working in context was critical. This means not identification of parts of speech but the actual use of words in real communication. Third, presentation of new material should be done utilizing key phrases that children can identify easily. Teachers should decide in advance what key phrases they want to utilize, and these should be emphasized constantly and consistently. Fourth, rhyme and movement are essential. As Rosanova (1998) indicated, young children love to sing and they love to move; rhythmic singing and movement are the physical embodiment of their capacity for memory. In terms of such multisensory learning, Goswami (2009) asserted that learning is multisensory and recommended that children be taught using a variety of their senses so that "learning will be stronger (that is, learning will be represented across a greater network of neurons, connecting a greater number of different neural structures, and accessible via a greater number of modalities)" (Kindle location 582).

Rosanova (1998) concluded that young children's growth to bilingualism was both resilient and robust under the right circumstances. In his view, the basic Montessori curriculum and standard Montessori practices supply the rudiments of what most children need. He further suggested that the three-to-six classrooms were an exceptionally good environment for the development of what, in second-language acquisition theory promoted by Jim Cummins (1999), was termed as basic interpersonal skills and cognitive academic language.

In *The Absorbent Mind*, Montessori (1949) presented her thoughts on language. She claimed that language grows in children organically, following natural developmental patterns that appear to be common to all children in all languages. Montessori asserted that from birth, children are engaged in developing the essential skills for whatever human language exists around them. Montessori also suggested that whether children's potential was limited to one language or was more fully developed depends very much on how early and how effectively children are exposed to other languages (Renton, 1998).

Reading and Writing

Rita Kramer (1988) noted that Montessori grew more and more interested in the possibility that the children in the Casa dei Bambini might be able to learn reading and writing effortlessly through methods similar to those

where they gained perceptual skills (making increasingly subtle discrimi-
nations of size, shape, pattern, and color by themselves). She thought
about the results of her work with deficient children, whom she had managed to teach to read and write using her three-dimensional models of
letters. This purposeful manipulation and movement in learning to read
and write was mentioned previously as being supported by neurological
research reported by Lillard (2008).

According to Kramer (1988), although it was not possible for Montessori to afford her three-dimensional original materials for the children in
the Casa dei Bambini, she herself elaborated letters that she cut out of
paper. Her assistants colored one set of letters blue, and she cut another
set out of sandpaper and glued these onto smooth cards. The children of
the Casa handled this sensorial apparatus (Montessori, 1955) and traced
the letter with their fingers and later with pencil or chalk, learning the
sounds, first vowels and then consonants. They took enormous pleasure
in the game by means of which they were teaching themselves what other
children two and three years older were learning so laboriously in the
regular school (Kramer, 1988).

The next accomplishment of the children of the Casa was reading,
which was learned after writing. This was contrary to the accepted idea
of the time. The children already knew the individual sounds of the letters. They put the sounds together and connected them with names of
things. This way, the children started to read from small slips on which
the names of familiar objects were written. Later, the children read short
sentences indicating actions to be performed. The small reading slips used
were brief, easy, clear, and at the same time interesting, especially as they
were also accompanied by motor activities, not of the hand only but of the
whole body (Kramer, 1988). As Kramer (1988) noted, the idea of children
four or five years old learning to write in less than two months and to read
in a few days was certainly revolutionary in 1907.

Montessori's Didactic Material

Guided by the work of Itard and Seguin, Montessori created a variety of
didactic materials. These materials did not represent Montessori's method
by themselves. As Montessori noted, these materials "became in the hands
of those who knew how to apply them, a most remarkable and efficient

means, but unless rightly presented, they failed to attract the attention of the [children]" (Montessori, 1964, p. 36).

Further, Montessori stated her belief that not the didactic materials but her voice "awakened the children, and encouraged them to use the didactic material and through it, to educate themselves" (Montessori, 1964, p. 37). Montessori's didactic materials were carefully designed to control every error, thus allowing the children to correct themselves. For example, a set of graduated wooden cylinders, as depicted in figure 5.2, control for the child's error. If the child places a cylinder into a hole that is too large, there will be a leftover cylinder at the end; thus, the child will know there is an error (Lillard, 2008).

Discipline

For Montessori, discipline came through liberty. She stated that "we call an individual disciplined when he was master of himself, and can, therefore, regulate his own conduct" (Montessori, 1964, p. 86). It is

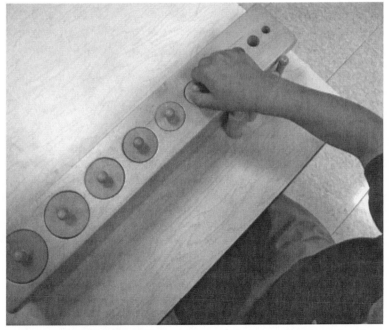

Figure 5.2. Child working with Montessori wooden cylinders. Irby photo used with permission.

through activity and movement that children learn to regulate their conduct and be independent. The children learn there is freedom to move about but that there is order in the classroom and the school and that responsibility is part of the freedom. Such an understanding of this discipline within the Montessori program is understood quickly as we have observed the program in weekly increments over the past ten years in a public school system. The discipline is closely associated with the social and emotions components and the sensorial period that relates to manners. With rules that are simple, the Montessori curriculum advocates teaching socially acceptable behavior and getting along with others. A young child will not automatically understand the abstract concept of respect.

Exercises of Practical Life

The Montessori Method includes exercises of practical life (cleanliness, order, poise, and conversation) performed at the beginning of the day. An inspection of cleanliness takes place as soon as children arrive at school. Teachers call the attention to the child in case of buttons missing, garments torn, or shoes not clean. It was expected that children "become accustomed to observing themselves and take an interest in their own appearance" (Montessori, 1964, p. 122).

Children are taught how to take care of themselves, and older children, should there be a mixed-age group, are taught to help the younger ones. After the previous exercise, the children proceed to put on their aprons and inspect the classroom. They make sure the materials are clean and in order. This is part of teaching respect and responsibility. When the children are ready with their materials in order, they are taught poise and equilibrium while sitting and working. Next, teachers invite the children to talk with them. These conversations among the children and the teacher "encouraged the unfolding or development of the language" and are also "of great educational value" (Montessori, 1964, p. 124), since children learn through such conversations proper conversational themes and ways to communicate with each other and with adults. Practical life activities in Montessori programs serve a purpose that is theoretically important, because "the action that occurs must be connected with the mental activity going on" (Montessori, 1967, p. 142).

Figure 5.3. Child in practical life center. Irby photo used with permission.

The practical life center contains everyday objects, as depicted in figure 5.3, that the children are familiar with and can manipulate. The purpose of this center is to provide exercises that develop within the child four primary skills: order, concentration, coordination, and independence.

It also teaches basic tasks that children must master to live comfortably in the adult world. The area is colorful and inviting, and children love to explore it. The practical life center prepares the child to read with the left-to-right/top-to-bottom concept; writing skills are enhanced by developing the pincer fingers; and math skills are developed by using logical thought, order, and sequence.

THE CASE: MONTESSORI, BILINGUAL, PRE-K PUBLIC SCHOOL, BRAIN-BASED EDUCATION

Presented herein is the case of a Montessori, bilingual, prekindergarten public school program in an urban school district in southeast Texas. As presented and discussed, carefully implemented Montessori Methods are instructionally brain compatible. This compatibility demonstrates the Montessori Method as one potential model for implementing brain-compatible learning, particularly at the early childhood and elementary grades. This a posteriori case was designed to address three specific questions utilizing applicable data from the Tejas LEE assessment tool.

First, we were interested in determining to what extent ELLs who participated in a Montessori prekindergarten program differ from ELLs who participated in a traditional prekindergarten program in the same district on a beginning-of-the-year statewide assessment of reading and language skills. To answer this question, data were collected from the Tejas LEE using 1,259 kindergarteners, among whom 479 had attended a Montessori prekindergarten program, and 780 had attended a traditional prekindergarten program in the same district in the prior year.

Second, we wanted to find out to what extent ELLs who participated in a Montessori prekindergarten program in an urban school district differ from ELLs who did not participate in a prekindergarten program in the same district on a beginning-of-the-year statewide assessment of reading and language skills upon entry into kindergarten in 2010. To answer this question, data were collected from the Tejas LEE using 1,017 kindergarteners, among whom 479 had participated in a Montessori prekindergarten program and 538 did not participate in a prekindergarten program.

Finally, we wanted to determine to what extent ELLs who participated in a Montessori prekindergarten program in an urban school district differ from ELLs who participated in a traditional prekindergarten program in the same district on a beginning-of-the-year statewide assessment of reading and language skills upon entry into kindergarten. Data for this question were collected from the Tejas LEE in 2011 using 180 kindergarteners from five campuses. Among these students, ninety students attended a traditional prekindergarten program in the urban school district, and a matched sample of ninety students (based on socioeconomic status, gender, and English-language proficiency level) from the respective campus were selected who attended a bilingual Montessori prekindergarten program in the same urban district in the 2010 academic year.

The school district personnel pulled all data for the two years of analysis. The analysis was performed in the district with no names of students accessible; only identifiable numbers for each student were analyzed. Native Spanish-speaking students were included in the sample.

Tejas LEE

The Tejas LEE is an assessment tool that measures student's reading, comprehension, and reading-related skills in Spanish from kindergarten through third grade. It helps teachers identify student's strengths and problem areas, monitor student progress over the course of the school year, and plan and deliver targeted instruction. The intent of Tejas LEE is to capture significant skills and steps in the development of Spanish reading and comprehension skills that can be used to plan individual or group reading instruction for early intervention and prevention of reading problems. The specific purposes of the Tejas LEE include the following:

- To provide an additional early Spanish reading instrument that districts may select and administer to fulfill the requirements of the Texas Education Code Section 28.006.
- To detect early reading difficulties or risk reading difficulties in Spanish reading at an early level, in grades K–3.
- To provide a summary of reading skills and comprehension, which teachers can use in planning individual or group instruction.

In kindergarten, the reading concepts addressed cover graphophonemic knowledge, phonological awareness, listening comprehension, and reading comprehension. The Tejas LEE includes three different performance levels of scoring to describe a student's level of skill/need on any section. The terms and definitions for each level are outlined below:

- Desarrollado (D) = The student has mastered the skill.
- Nivel esperado (NE) = The student is performing at a level expected for that grade and time point. In some instances, students may score NE but not D, meaning they are expected to further develop this skill during the remainder of the school year. In such a case, a score equivalent to NE is acceptable and should not be considered problematic.
- Nivel de intervención (NI) = The student is performing below the expected level for the grade level and time point. Intervention is strongly recommended.

The Prekindergarten, Montessori, Bilingual Program

The prekindergarten Montessori Center is a public school supported through federal funds. Some 89 percent of the children were identified at the poverty level. Of the 858 children on the campus, 85.5 percent were Hispanic; 10.3 percent, African American; and 4 percent, other. Some 71 percent of the children were categorized as ELL and were served in bilingual classrooms (Texas Education Agency, 2011). The prekindergarten Montessori Center, opened in the fall of 1998, was a result of the school district's successful passage of a $20 million bond election to support the building of four early childhood centers. A forty-thousand-square-foot urban campus, the center housed eighteen classrooms, a multipurpose room, a library, a teacher workroom, a lounge, a nurse's station, a parent workroom, a diagnostician office, a counseling room, a speech therapy room, and an office area. Each classroom was equipped with its own lavatory, drinking fountain, and sink. Twelve classrooms were in open areas, while six were self-contained. Nine of the classrooms were designated as bilingual classrooms (five self-contained; four open). The campus sits on the corner of a busy Houston intersection and is surrounded by a grass-covered playground. On one side of the campus is a wooded area, on another side is a large church, and on the other side is a large Hispanic flea market. The eight elementary campuses from which the sample was drawn were located within a five-mile radius of the center. None of the elementary campuses continued the Montessori program in kindergarten, first, or second grade.

At the Montessori Center, each classroom is equipped fully with quality Montessori materials, more than is observed in many private school Montessori classrooms. Each classroom has new materials that are well cared for by the teacher and the students, because in the Montessori environment everything has its proper place and must be kept in order. Each classroom cost is at least $40,000. Materials, many three-dimensional and multisensory, are arranged in centers. Each center is correlated to the curriculum that is sequential, integrated, and aligned to the state standards for prekindergarten (PK), the district benchmarks, and the Montessori Methodology and philosophy.

Each teacher in the Montessori Center is certified by the state. In addition, each teacher receives five weeks of mandatory Montessori training from the National Center for Montessori Education at a cost of $5,000 per teacher. Training continues throughout the following school year with a certified trainer with ongoing curriculum and instructional support. In Montessori, the teacher is trained to prepare an environment responsive to the needs of the learner and to prepare the learners to meet their own needs and encourage conversation with the children. These conversations among the children and the teacher encourage the unfolding, or development, of the language. A Montessori teacher is also trained to teach the children how to have poise, order, and equilibrium while working in centers or individually. Lessons in the Montessori Method are individualized, concise, simple, objective, and allow for teacher observation.

Teachers are trained to observe and take records. The teacher is trained to develop a classroom focused on creating a love of order; love of work; profound spontaneous concentration; attachment to reality; the love of silence and of working alone; sublimation of the possessive instinct; power to act from real choice and not from curiosity, obedience, independence, and initiative; spontaneous self-discipline; and joy. The teaching staff and administrators share a common educational philosophy and have collaboratively developed expected levels of students' achievement with daily observations and formal assessments conducted every three weeks.

Montessori training is intensive and imparts an attitude as well as information. The training includes Montessori child psychology, educational theory, material demonstrations, supervised practice with Montessori materials, observation of Montessori classrooms, supervised practiced teaching, and extensive written and oral exams. Multiaged clusters enhance the Montessori dynamic by reducing competition, maximizing curriculum options available to any one child, providing a family atmosphere that plays a vital role in socialization, and permitting older children to model advanced work for younger children.

The Montessori Center takes a holistic approach to educating the child. Parents are trained in the Montessori philosophy and are required to volunteer time at the school. The school is welcoming, and over twenty thousand volunteer hours are logged annually. The principal at the PK, Montessori, bilingual program makes every effort to (a) recruit highly qualified, bilingual early childhood teachers; (b) provide additional training and other support to ensure student achievement success; (c) offer time for teachers to plan together; and (d) create a collective awareness among teachers about their reading program in Spanish.

The three PK traditional bilingual centers, centers A, B, and C, were funded with federal funds that support low-income children. In center A, 96.3 percent of the student population was economically disadvantaged. Sixty-six of the children were categorized as ELL. Of the 595 children on the campus, 78 percent were Hispanic; 18 percent, African American; and 2 percent, other. In center B, 94 percent of the student population was economically disadvantaged. Of the six hundred children on the campus, 95 percent were Hispanic; 2 percent, African American; and 3 percent, other, while 66 percent of the children were categorized as ELL. In center C, 96.4 percent of the student population was economically disadvantaged. Of the 557 children on the campus, 64.6 percent were Hispanic; 32.3 percent, African American; and 2.1 percent, other. Some 49 percent of the children were categorized as ELL (TEA, 2011).

WHAT WE LEARNED

The analysis of data utilized a chi-square test performed on each subtest to compare the percentage of students' performance level identified as developed on Tejas LEE, and effect sizes for the magnitude of statistical significance were reported in the form of Cramer's V. We learned several critical things pertaining to our brain-compatible Montessori program.

First, we learned there was a statistically significant difference between the two groups previously defined on three subtests in the areas of phonological awareness and graphophonemic knowledge. Post hoc analysis revealed that ELLs who participated in a Montessori prekindergarten program outperformed those who participated in a traditional prekindergarten program in initial sound identification and decoding/single word reading (see figure 5.4).

Next, we found a statistically significant difference between the two groups on seven subtests in the areas of book and print awareness, phonological awareness, and graphophonemic knowledge. Post hoc analysis revealed that all the significance was in favor of children who participated in a Montessori prekindergarten program, indicating that they demonstrated higher levels of Spanish preliteracy skills than did those who did not participate in a prekindergarten program (see figure 5.5).

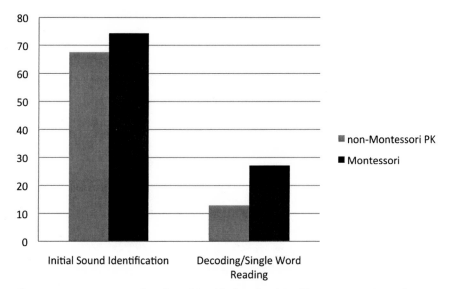

Figure 5.4. Percentage of students identified as developed between non-PK and Montessori PK, 2010.

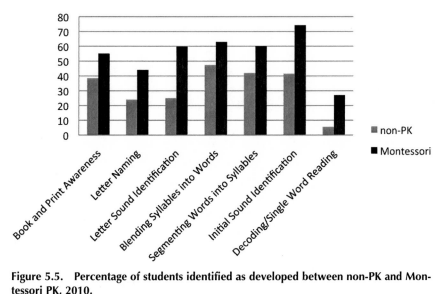

Figure 5.5. Percentage of students identified as developed between non-PK and Montessori PK, 2010.

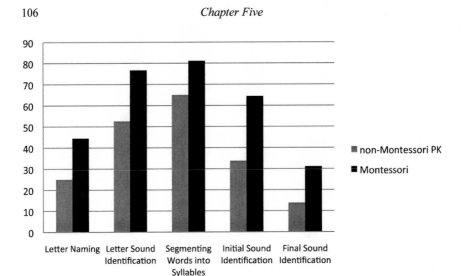

Figure 5.6. Percentage of students identified as developed between non-PK and Montessori PK, 2011.

Finally, we were not surprised to find that a statistically significant difference was identified between the two groups on five subtests in the areas of phonological awareness and graphophonemic knowledge. A post hoc analysis revealed that all the significance was in favor of ELLs who participated in a Montessori prekindergarten, indicating that they demonstrated higher levels of Spanish preliteracy skills than did those who participated in a traditional prekindergarten program (see figure 5.6).

Obviously those findings were exciting, and we were further enthused about the implications of those data and how we could use them in our program to help inform other parts of the instruction program in the district. In the back of our minds, we also felt we were onto something (i.e., the brain compatibility of the Montessori Method) not well documented in the literature. We believe that other educators can benefit from these findings or lessons, which ultimately means that other children can benefit equally as much as the children in our case.

RELATING BRAIN-BASED EDUCATION TO THE CASE

We found, in our case study, that ELLs who participated in a Montessori prekindergarten program experienced greater achievement in reading-

related skills in their native language than did those ELLs who participated in a traditional prekindergarten program, and such an advantage was
even more evident when those Montessori ELLs were compared to other
ELLs who did not have the opportunity to participate in any prekindergarten program. We observed that for ELLs from low socioeconomic status
families, their potential was influenced deeply at the Montessori prekindergarten school, where their native language was practiced, advanced,
and respected. Further, ELLs benefited from the early exposure to both
languages during the prekindergarten period, defined by Montessori as the
second stage of the epoch of the absorbent mind, or by Helfrich (2011)
who noted the sensitive period for language that specifically facilitates
learning consciously from the environment and eventually the language
acquisition (Sousa, 2010b).

These findings support the Montessori philosophy that when children
are exposed to a rich environment in which they can practice language
and engage in language, the brain development, or more specifically, the
linguistic potential, can be activated and accelerated (Renton, 1998). We
agree with Renton (1998) that it is critical for maintaining and developing the home language of culturally and linguistically diverse learners as
fully as possible, because primary language skills in a first language are
the basis for developing skills in a second language. Taken together, the
implementation of the Montessori model in the prekindergarten year is
beneficial for a child's brain to efficiently acquire and learn a wide range
of language and prereading skills in particular.

INFORMING YOUR PRACTICE: BUILDING
A BRAIN-COMPATIBLE ENVIRONMENT

If educational leaders want to take the information from this case and
build a brain-compatible environment, they should consider the following five actions. Though our case included English-language learners, we
believe that there are many children from impoverished backgrounds who
are also at a loss in terms of English-language skills. Also, the Montessori
Method, as we have observed it over a decade, can enhance brain development among all children.

- Action 1. Develop early childhood programs that have a Montessori philosophical base. This means engaging children in authentic learning environments where the native language is practiced, developed, and respected and where brain-compatible learning is naturally incorporated into the curriculum.
- Action 2. Develop both languages at the early learning grade levels. The dual-language development occurs during Montessori's sensitive period or epoch during the time when children are able to acquire a second language with ease.
- Action 3. Provide a culturally and linguistically relevant environment in which the child can engage in oral language development and dialogue as opposed to an environment in which teachers do most of the talking. Such a language-rich, child-centered environment advances brain development and enhances language acquisition.
- Action 4. Have students engage all of their senses in learning. Sensorial learning environments enhance brain development and promote active learning. Relatedly, learning styles of students should be included in the sensorial learning environment. The environment should be a place where students can explore and learn with language developed via the senses.
- Action 5. Provide professional development for teachers that includes (a) information about brain-based learning; (b) emotional relationships to learning; (c) effective learning environments that are language rich and stimulating; (d) sensorial input into learning; (e) motivation and respect for self and others, which relates to collaborative learning; (f) organization in the classroom; and (g) relating the learning actions to language development and second-language acquisition strategies. Provide time for professional development and follow-up for the teachers.

In order for administrators to inform their own leadership with brain-based strategies, they themselves must engage in learning about how brain-based research and learning principles may be included in school environments. Additionally, those administrators who serve large numbers of English-language learners should take into account the five basic actions based on the findings of this Montessori, bilingual, prekindergarten case in order to develop language and literacy skills in their students.

Our most critical action is action 1, as it relates directly to our case study. In our case, we observed positive effects of bilingual education under the Montessori Method that are very closely linked to brain-based enhanced learning. Our case results indicate that prekindergarten, Montessori, bilingual education for native Spanish-speaking ELLs can activate and enhance brain development in the native language. Therefore, it seems that it would behoove administrators who specifically work in heavily populated native Spanish-speaking districts to support a public school, Montessori, bilingual education at the prekindergarten level, and for those who do not work in such districts, it still seems that the findings and lessons that have emerged from our Montessori case should lend encouragement to any leader who wants to lay a strong foundation for the academic achievement for all children.

REFERENCES

Bruer, J. T. (1997). Education and the brain: A bridge too far. *Educational Researcher, 26*(8), 4–16.

Caine, R. N., & Caine, G. (2011). *Natural for a connected world: Education, technology and the human brain*. New York: Teachers College Press.

Caine, R. N., & Caine, G. (1997). *Education on the edge of possibility*. Alexandria, VA: Association for Supervision and Curriculum Development.

Caine, R. N., & Caine, G. (1994). *Making connections: Teaching and the human brain*. New York: Addison-Wesley Publishers.

Cummins, J. (1999). BICS and CALP: Clarifying the distinction. University of Toronto, Opinion Papers 120. Retrieved from http://ezproxy.wou.edu:2100/hww/results/external_link_maincontentframe.jhtml?_DARGS=/hww/results/results_common.jhtml.44.

Goswami, U. (2009). Principals of learning, implications for teaching: A cognitive neuroscience. In R. Cigman & A. Davis (Eds.), *New philosophies of learning* (pp. 26–43). Chichester, UK: Wiley/Blackwell.

Helfrich, M. S. (2011). *Montessori learning in the 21st century: A guide for parents and teachers*. Troutdale, OR: Newsage Press.

Hileman, S. (2006). Motivating students using brain-based teaching strategies. *Agricultural Education Magazine, 78*(4), 18–20.

Immordino-Yang, M. H., & Matthias, F. (2010). Building smart students: A neuroscience perspective on the role of emotion and skilled intuition in learning. In D.A.Sousa, (ed.), *The Future of Educational Neuroscience: Where We Are Now, and Where We're Going Next*. Bloomington, IN: Solution Tree Press.

Jensen, E. (2008). *Brain-based learning: The new paradigm of teaching*. Thousand Oaks, CA: Corwin.

Kramer, R. (1976). *Maria Montessori.* New York: G.P. Putman's Sons.

Kramer, R. M. (1988). *Maria Montessori: A Biography.* Reading, MA: Addison-Wesley.

Krashen, S. (1988). Providing input for acquisition. In P. A. Richard-Amato (Ed.), *Making it happen: Interaction in the second language classroom from theory to practice* (pp. 330–342). White Plains, NY: Longman.

Lillard, A. S. (2008). *Montessori: The science behind the genius.* New York: Oxford University Press.

Lillard, A. S., & Else-Quest, N. (2006). Evaluating Montessori education. *Science, 313,* 1893–1894. Retrieved from http://montessori.org.au/research/ScienceLillard060929.pdf.

Lillard, P., & Jessen, L. L. (2003). *Montessori from the start: The child, from birth to age three.* New York: Schocken Books.

Montessori, M. (1967). *The discovery of the child.* New York: Ballantine.

Montessori, M. (1964). *The Montessori method.* New York: Shocken Books.

Montessori, M. (1955). *The formation of man.* Theosophical Publishing House, Adyar.

Montessori, M. (1949). *The absorbent mind.* Radford, VA: Wilder Publications.

Montessori, M. (1917). *The advanced Montessori method: The Montessori elementary material,* tr. by A. Livingston. New York: Frederick A. Stokes Company.

Montessori, M. (1914). *Dr. Montessori's own handbook.* New York: Shocken Books.

Montessori, M. (1913). *Pedagogical anthropology.* New York: Frederick A. Stokes.

Montessori, M. (1912). *The Montessori Method.* Translated by Anne Everett George. New York: Frederick A. Stokes.

O'Keefe, J., & Nadel, L. (1978). *The hippocampus as a cognitive map.* Oxford, England: Clarendon Press.

Petitto, L. A., Katerelos, M., Levy, B. G., Gauna, K., Tétreault, K., & Ferraro, V. (2001). Bilingual signed and spoken language acquisition from birth: Implications for the mechanisms underlying early bilingual language acquisition. *Journal of Child Language, 28*(2), 453–496.

Rao, H., Betancourt, L., Giannetta, J. M., Brodsky, N. L., Korczykowski, M., Avants, B. B., Gee, J. C., Wang, J., Hurt, H., Detre, J. A., & Farah, M. J. (2010). Early parental care is important for hippocampal maturation: Evidence from brain morphology in humans. *NeuroImage, 49,* 1144–1150.

Redlinger, W., & Park, T. Z. (1980). Language mixing in young bilingual children. *Journal of Child Language, 7*(1), 24–30.

Renton, A. M. (1998). Cultivating the natural linguist. *Montessori Life, 10*(2), 31–33.

Rippa, S. A. (1997). *Education in a free society* (8th ed.). New York: Longman.

Rodriguez, L., Irby, B., Brown, G., Lara-Alecio, R., & Galloway, M. (2005). An analysis of second grade reading achievement related to pre-kindergarten Montessori and transitional bilingual education. *Review of Research and Practice, 3*, 45–65.

Rosanova, M. (1998). Early childhood bilingualism in the Montessori Children's House: Guessable context and the planned environment. Spotlight: Montessori—Multilingual, Multicultural. *Montessori Life, 10*(2), 37¬–48.

Rothbart, M. K., Posner, M. I., Rueda, M. R., Sheese, B. E., & Tang, Y.-Y. (2009). Enhancing self-regulation in school and clinic. In D. Cicchetti & M. R. Gunnar (Eds.), *Minnesota symposium on child psychology: Meeting the challenge of translational research in child psychology* (pp. 115–158). Hoboken, NJ: Wiley.

Shaw, P., Greenstein, D., Lerch, J., Clasen, L., Lenroot, R., Gogtay, N., Evans, A., Rapoport, J., & Giedd, J. (2006). Intellectual ability and cortical development in children and adolescents. *Nature, 440*, 676–679.

Sousa, D. A. (2011). *How the brain learns* (4th ed.). Thousand Oaks, CA: Corwin.

Sousa, D. A. (2010a). *How the ELL brain learns*. Thousand Oaks, CA: Sage.

Sousa, D. A. (2010b). *Mind, brain, and education: Neuroscience implications for the classroom*. Bloomington, IN: Solution Trees Press.

Standing, E. M. (1957). *Maria Montessori: Her life and work*. New York: Plume.

Texas Education Agency (TEA). (2011). 2010–11 academic excellence indicator system. Retrieved from http://ritter.tea.state.tx.us/perfreport/aeis/2011/index.html.

Tomlinson, C. A., & Sousa, D. A. (2011). *Differentiation and the brain: How neuroscience supports the learner-friendly classroom*. Bloomington, IN: Solution Trees Press.

Vihman, M. (1985). Language differentiation by the bilingual infant. *Journal of Child Language, 12*(2), 297–324.

Williams, D. L. (2010). The speaking brain. In D. Sousa (Ed.), *Mind, brain, and education: Neuroscience implications for the classroom* (Leading Edge Series; Kindle location 1756–1757). Bloomington, IN: Solution Tree Press.

Willis, J. (2010). The current impact of neuroscience on teaching and learning. In D. Sousa (Ed.), *Mind, brain, and education: Neuroscience implications for the classroom* (Leading Edge Series; Kindle location 1034–1038). Bloomington, IN: Solution Tree Press.

Chapter Six

Launch of Apollo

Brain-Compatible Algebra

Camille Malone

Now is an exciting and pivotal time to be an educator. Neuroimaging and brain mapping research has extended beyond the confines of studying medical and psychological diseases and has opened windows into the brain. We can now see brain activity as information from the senses that is categorized and organized into working, relational, and, ultimately, long-term memories. In short, we can now see what happens to brain activity and structure when teachers teach and when students learn. Educators can now relate the powerful discoveries of learning brain research to classrooms and curriculum by incorporating research-based learning strategies to help students learn more effectively and joyfully. The potential for discovering the most effective ways to educate students is unlimited.

—Judy Willis (2006)

A few years into the new century, the Dallas Independent School District (DISD) welcomed a new superintendent, and in the summer of that year, he brought to the district a curriculum and instruction leader who began to point us in a significant new direction, one that I had never experienced as an educator. As the executive director of mathematics, I had an integral role in leading the district in both the study and the application of current educational research in mathematics curriculum. In addition, I was responsible for providing teacher professional development for the implementation of research-based strategies in the delivery of mathematics instruction. My central mathematics team included eight specialists—four elementary, two middle, and two high school—each of whom supervised several instructional coaches. Thus, the district mathematics department was a team of approximately fifty who served all the mathematics teachers, and their administrators, in the 160,000-student-strong Dallas ISD. Little did I know (little did we know) that after more than twenty-five years in the classroom, I was about to take a journey, taking my team with me, that would confirm all our intuitive beliefs about mathematics teaching and learning. This is the story of that journey, including the significant events that influenced our direction, the lessons that we learned, and the reasons for the decisions we made along the way. I share this personal case study with the hope that fellow educators will see the importance of what we discovered and the significance of what happened, and be able to apply it to their own situations. This shared experience can be especially useful in a high school setting where we found that, indeed, a research-based, brain-based curriculum and instruction protocol can be developed and implemented resulting in students successfully learning Algebra I—and having fun doing it!

EXAMINING THE "WHAT" TO TEACH

Like most teachers, we had been teaching mathematics as we were instructed, following a prescribed sequence of topics on a time line, without really considering the content. However, in the fall, the district began a close examination of the "what" we were teaching to our students in mathematics, as well as the other core curriculum areas (science, English and language arts, and social studies). The National Council of Teachers of Mathematics (NCTM) had published *Curriculum and Evaluation Standards for School Mathematics* in March of 1989, and the mathematics arm of our state's Texas Education Agency (TEA) had become a national leader in the development of very comprehensive state mathematics standards based on those of the NCTM. The state standards, published for every grade level and course in mathematics, were titled the Texas Essential Knowledge and Skills (TEKS), and each standard, or TEKS, had subcategories called Student Expectations (SEs) that were the concepts, understandings, and skills that every student should master. For example, the following was amended to be effective in 2006, for Algebra I,

TEKS (A.1). Foundations for functions. "The student understands that a function represents a dependence of one quantity on another and can be described in a variety of ways." And,

SE (A.1) (B), "The student is expected to gather and record data and use data sets to determine functional relationships between quantities."

Additionally, TEA implemented a process whereby Texas state standards for all subjects were systematically and periodically reviewed and revised as necessary, and some of the current TEKS could be somewhat amended from those in use at that time. However, the basic concepts to be taught in mathematics remained largely unchanged.

At the district level, as part of that examination of the "what," the mathematics department was directed to examine the Texas standards for coherence, depth, and complexity, as well as fidelity to the intent of the NCTM standards. Our process and our findings proved to be quite an eye-opening experience. I assigned my team the task of copying and laminating each SE individually, so that each grade level and each high school course had about thirty separate laminated SEs. I also assigned one or two team members to be responsible for the SEs of each grade or course to keep them separate, and then we began a process of "discovery."

I gathered the mathematics supervisors and instructional coaches in a large room with three blank walls, all well illuminated by a fourth wall of very tall windows. I asked the kindergarten team to begin taping the first TEKS/SE (K.1) (A) to the top of the wall on the left side. To the right of it, the first-grade team aligned TEKS/SE (1.1) (A) and taped it up. The next group put up the TEKS/SE that would logically follow the conceptual sequence in second grade, and so on. Of course, since mathematics content does not follow the same vertical sequence in each grade level, the horizontal sequence from grade level to grade level began to veer from the pattern of (K.1) (A) to (1.1) (A) and (2.1) (A), and so forth. Nevertheless, we soon were astonished to find that there were instances of a significant lack of coherence from grade level to grade level. For instance, we saw a large gap in the content from grade five to six to grade eight, and perhaps not quite as surprising, from grade seven to Algebra I, typically the ninth-grade mathematics course for most students. We also noted several grade levels/courses where a lack of coherence in content seemed to correlate with lower state achievement scores. Having laid out the entire system of state mathematics standards from kindergarten to precalculus, we began the work of carefully filling in the gaps we had identified.

We added language to some standards where we thought necessary. We also created and added entire local DISD standards in order to begin concept development earlier, to bridge gaps from one grade level to another, and to extend consideration of a concept into the next grade level or course through review and additional application. Further, we added depth and complexity to those standards where appropriate in order to better support and enhance student learning. For example, for the Algebra I TEKS/SE (A.1) (B) shown previously, we added the phrase "and analyze" in order to emphasize the importance of analyzing the critical attributes of functional relationships, perhaps through class discussion, rather than simply having students answer problems through some procedural routine without understanding the mathematical meanings. Our local standard then read, "The student is expected to gather and record data and use data sets, to determine and analyze functional relationships between quantities."

Our goal was multifold. It was a given that we wanted to meet the state standards requirements, but in addition, we aimed to exceed the basic requirements, or as our superintendent called it, the "floor." We wanted to aim for the "ceiling" for our students, and that goal was to facilitate their mastery of the mathematics necessary for college or career readiness.

We spent several weeks adding language to the state TEKS/SEs to create the "Dallas ISD Mathematics Standards," but once the document was completed, we had what we believed to be the most coherent, aligned, and conceptually complete set of standards in existence, both vertically and horizontally, around which to build mathematics curriculum. We were ready for the next step, that of creating curriculum guides for our teachers based on the more comprehensive standards. Our previous curriculum documents had followed our textbooks, but now, in addition, we would create lessons for the changes we had made to our content standards.

DISCIPLINARY LITERACY

At the same time the other curriculum departments were examining and revising standards that fall, the district began collaborating with the Institute for Learning (IFL) at the University of Pittsburgh. The IFL was founded by Lauren Resnick, renowned cognitive psychologist, to facilitate educational practitioners in achieving the goals of the standards movement and to bridge research and practice (Institute for Learning, 2009–2012). Based on IFL research, we also initiated a new era of professional development that included central curriculum personnel and district teachers of core subjects, particularly math and language arts. Rather than a standard didactic training, each and every session began with all the participants, teachers, central instructional staff members, and selected administrators reading and dissecting an article based on current educational research.

The first was a study of "Leadership for Learning: A Theory of Action for Urban School Districts" (Resnick & Glennan, 2002). After careful reading, we had intense text-based discussions, and the participating teachers enthusiastically provided input from their classroom experiences. We began to see a much larger and more comprehensive picture of the educational problems across the nation. We learned that districts should be organized around instruction and learning, a prospect reflected in the heart of every classroom teacher, and we began to focus on possibilities for change in Dallas ISD.

We also examined "Making America Smarter" (Resnick, 1999). Studying this article led us to take a fresh look at our beliefs about intelligence and whether, through effort and rich learning opportunities, every student could succeed. We engaged in deep and extended study of a core set of principles that guided the work of the Institute for Learning: the Principles of Learning (POLs; University of Pittsburgh, 2005). We noted that the research called for a math classroom characterized by students in collaborative socialized settings, engaged in problem solving and discussion around mathematical concepts, rather than a classroom with the teacher on a proverbial stage.

Another major focus of our study was the idea of disciplinary literacy. Decades ago, Jerome Bruner (1960) argued that the goal of mathematics should be to help students think mathematically; that is, to practice the habits of thinking as a mathematician by engaging in reasoning, conjecturing, testing, discussing, and problem solving. Disciplinary literacy, as defined by the IFL, is mastery of both the core concepts and the habits of thinking of a discipline (Institute for Learning, 2006). As we mulled over these ideas, we came to believe that our students would flourish in a disciplinary literacy classroom, an environment where they could often work together in groups to solve problems through mathematical reasoning, facilitated by their teacher, of course. Our ideas about what constituted quality curriculum and instruction changed radically, and we became more and more optimistic about what we could do for our students. The possibilities seemed to be endless.

Several district administrators, including curriculum directors, attended the first of a series of semiannual workshops with IFL instructors, and five of my staff members attended the winter IFL conference with me in Pittsburgh in 2008. For three days, we were immersed in the mathematics education research. We were particularly struck by videos of classrooms where teachers, rather than presenting content, facilitated groups of students who were discussing mathematics as they collaboratively worked on math tasks. On our evening flight returning to Dallas, one of the high school supervisors said that if we did not create and implement a "Disciplinary Literacy" (DL) curriculum, we would never impact student achievement in the way that had been described and observed. I had been thinking the same thing for several months, and now, we all recognized the significant possibilities that came from the educational studies of leading academicians. I began thinking about algebra in particular.

THE CRISIS IN ALGEBRA

Educators and educational researchers have commonly called high school algebra a gateway course for several reasons. Primarily, algebra proficiency provides entrance into higher-level secondary mathematics coursework (Educational Testing Service, 2009; Matthews & Farmer, 2008; National Council of Teachers of Mathematics, 1989; RAND Corporation, 2003; U.S. Department of Education, 1997). Also, as a consequence of mastering algebra and attaining higher levels of mathematics coursework, students have access to an increased number of, and higher quality of, career opportunities (Stapel, 2006–2009). It follows that limitations of career opportunities for any section of the population have significant social implications. "Failure to learn algebra is widespread, and the consequences of this failure are that far too many students are disenfranchised. This curtailment of opportunity falls most directly upon groups that are already disadvantaged and exacerbates existing inequalities in our society" (RAND Corporation, 2003, p. xx). Robert Moses and Charles Cobb (2001) proposed that algebra was the new civil right and as such it should be accessible to everyone. As a former calculus teacher, I knew firsthand the importance of algebra. I desperately wanted to find a way so that algebra was not only accessible to every single student in the district but was also a course in which our students excelled.

As I was thinking about what a disciplinary literacy classroom in algebra would look like, a scene from the movie *Apollo 13* came to my mind. The scene centered on a crisis: the astronauts were running out of oxygen. Back on earth, the ground crew members at NASA gathered in a room and were told of the emergency. Duplicates of all the equipment that was available to the astronauts in space was dumped on a large table, and the engineers, scientists, and mathematicians were challenged to use that equipment, and nothing else, to solve the problem and save the lives of the three astronauts. They began to examine the stuff on the table, and I imagined that they would talk intensely and urgently with one another, certainly conjecture and argue about what would work and what wouldn't, and test possible solutions, probably many, many times. They would keep on until they had solved the problem. I thought, "That's disciplinary literacy in action!" We would name our new algebra curriculum Apollo!

WHAT'S BEST FOR STUDENTS? TO DO OR NOT TO DO

I had already contemplated the ramifications of doing what we knew was best for our students. A school district is a political system, and a large city district has all the characteristics and personalities of any political system: those who will put the education of children first and work diligently to help teachers and principals accomplish the best for students; those who seek power and recognition for themselves regardless of the outcome on education; and those who, for some other reason, will negate any ideas, suggestions, or even authentic research that would help children. If we chose to create a DL curriculum in algebra, it could mean challenging many of the stakeholders in the district. I had reached the "magic" number of years so that I could retire, but I had to consider my high school team, none of whom was vested. I thought long and hard about that challenge. How long do you accept incremental growth in student achievement in algebra as the norm year after year? How long do you keep doing the same thing you have done before? How long do you read and study research and review case studies where student learning is remarkable and do nothing? I thought it had been long enough.

I met with the high school team and told them my thoughts, concerns, and goals, and I told them about the work that would be involved for them, particularly. Our instructional coaches spent Monday through

Thursday on their campuses, primarily helping teachers, and Fridays, the day for our own professional development, would be the only weekday we had for creating curriculum. However, there were notable factors that were favorable for making the project work. Several of the instructional coaches had been engineers before they were teachers (I hired former engineers every chance I could), and I, and my supervisors, had brought all of the research training we had experienced the last three years back to them as it occurred. Also, all of them had extensive and significant expertise in secondary mathematical content, and of course, they had been hired because of the high achievement of their students. They were excellent classroom teachers.

I explained that the work would be intense and exhaustive, but maybe, possibly, it would be one of our most rewarding educational experiences, and more so for our teachers and students. They agreed that the place to begin, if we began, was in first-year algebra. As they listened, they looked at one another, realizing the gravity of what I had presented to them. I began to hear comments like, "That would be so awesome, so much better for our students; it would be incredible," and "Let's try it," and finally, "We can do it. We're in." What a remarkable team of educators! They realized that they had only the remainder of the spring semester and summer to create a research-based algebra curriculum for the coming year, like none they had seen, and everyone was on board. They agreed that the work would be very difficult and time consuming, and they agreed that it was the only ethical pathway we could take for our students, knowing what we knew! My email slogan became, "Why Apollo? Because to do otherwise would be to ignore research and fail our students." None of us realized the challenges ahead, the pitfalls and frustrations inherent in such an effort, or the joy over the triumphs of student success.

LEAVING THE TEXTBOOK BEHIND

Mathematics educators create lessons, practice worksheets for class and homework, and many, many types of assessments. But the question was, "How do we create an entire, coherent, disciplinary literacy and brain-based algebra curriculum?" No publisher had created the curriculum we envisioned for algebra. There were sets of various types of problems available and suggestions for student collaboration during problem solving. There were excellent examples of case studies with students working on tasks, but we knew of no entire curriculum, no blueprint or model. We began to think about what resources were available to us, and we looked for a textbook built on disciplinary literacy ideas.

Some members of the math team had provided input to textbook publishers during their careers. University mathematicians, math directors, specialists, and classroom teachers, among others, are often elicited to write chapters, sections, or individual lessons or to edit, or provide feedback, in the creation of textbooks. The result is a text, a resource that is used to support classroom instruction. In fact, research indicates that for the majority of teachers, the textbook is actually utilized as the curriculum (Clements, 2003; Kieran, 1992; Senk, 1989; Seymour & Davidson, 2003). Further, the American Association for the Advancement of Science (2000) in an extensive review of mathematics textbooks found a significant lack of strategies for effectively facilitating student understanding of algebra.

Therefore, based on current research, we believed that a DL algebra curriculum could not be implemented with a traditional textbook. Problem solving involves actually solving a mathematical problem. Inherent in actual problem solving should be confusion, questioning, hypothesizing, exploring pathways to solutions, and finally figuring out an answer (or multiple answers). It is not, and cannot be, working twenty problems in class or at home, after a teacher has explained and illustrated the procedure and solution steps for working them from a textbook. In that all-to-common scenario, students are performing rote procedural skills with little or no challenge. "'Thinking' is not the same thing as 'getting answers'" (ARISE, 1998, p. v). And following textbook procedures for getting answers is certainly not problem solving. Since a research-based curriculum program like we wanted had not been published, we would create our own, with limited use of the textbook.

BUY-IN FROM THE BIGWIGS

I presented our plan for creating and teaching a disciplinary literacy mathematics curriculum in Algebra I to the district curriculum and instruction administrator. I explained that we would be implementing all that we had learned in the past three years from research, particularly from the Institute for Learning. I also explained that research indicated that textbooks often functioned as a source of lessons and homework (Donoghue, 2003) and that it would be very difficult to retain the textbook as a primary teaching resource while at the same time attempting to implement a disciplinary literacy curriculum. I gave assurance that we would use our textbook when appropriate, but in order to teach a research-based algebra curriculum we would use the text more as a homework resource than as a lesson source. The idea of a DL algebra course was met with enthusiasm. Next, my project manager and I met with the district's three Learning Community administrators for secondary schools and told them of our plan. They had been deeply involved as an integral part of our work with the IFL, so I hoped that they would be very enthusiastic to support our new research-based direction. One administrator was supportive. It was time to begin creating curriculum.

ALGEBRA CONTENT IN SEQUENCE

The first question was, "What should be taught in a high school algebra course?" Unfortunately, there was substantial research indicating that assessment was driving curriculum (Clements, 2003; Jones, 2009). In Texas, student mastery of the state standards was measured by the Texas Assessment of Knowledge and Skills (TAKS). While we wanted to aim for the ceiling for our students by developing algebraic concepts in a comprehensive course that was not based on any particular assessment, it was imperative that we teach inclusive of the state curriculum and teach it well. After all, in addition to ensuring the best for the students, evaluations on our principals, teachers, and many administrators were based primarily on student state assessment data.

Thus, to begin, we copied, cut out, and laminated all released grade nine TAKS problems from past years in order to study how each standard and Student Expectation was tested. We made a poster for each standard and organized all the test problems on the posters that we thought were appropriate. In a few cases, we disagreed with the state. In other words, TEA may have listed TAKS problem 3 as an item that tested TEKS/SE (A.2) (C), and we aligned it under another SE.

At the same time, we began to study texts that were unfamiliar to us, resources from the University of Texas at Austin Dana Center, and other resources in order to create a sequence of algebra topics. We had studied the work of Lev Vygotsky (1978), and it was of paramount importance to us to make sure that we created a "zone of proximal development" that led seamlessly from one topic to another. As expert classroom teachers, many of the staff disagreed with our current textbook sequence, but they also often disagreed with one another. We created afternoon discussion groups, and we talked about the content, the concepts, and the meaning of every topic, and where each fit in the larger sequence. There was a two-week period when an ongoing heated discussion of the meaning of "rate" versus "rate of change" nearly sabotaged the entire project. But we were determined to never, ever create curriculum with mathematical flaws. We made absolutely sure of our definitions and the conceptual presentations, and we carefully vetted every word. No one came to blows . . . and we continued.

The work was innovative and hard, the team was new and untried, and compromise was not always natural to secondary certified mathematics instructors. It was significantly more difficult to create a curriculum from scratch than to write a scope and sequence based on a textbook that is in use in the classroom every day. After a few weeks, we agreed upon the best sequence for learning Algebra I topics. Next, it was time to begin creating curriculum units!

LEARNING TASKS AND SOCIAL CONTEXT

In the last two decades, brain research began to focus more heavily on learning, and findings gained more legitimacy when neuroscientists, using brain-imaging technology during the learning process, provided strategies for more effective teaching (Willis, 2006). In addition, two instructional strategies have been, and continue to be, exceptionally prominent in mathematics educational cognitive research, each of which is also considered a major focus in brain-learning research. The first is the concept of "task." The centuries-old debate between telling content to students versus facilitating problem solving through a task that embodies the mathematical concept is essentially coming to an end. The research is overwhelming.

The 1991 NCTM standards recommended that students be engaged in interactive mathematical activity grounded in rich, challenging, worthwhile mathematical tasks. Walter Doyle and Kathy Carter (1984) stated, "Tasks organize cognition" (p. 130), and Mary Kay Stein, Barbara Grover, and Marjorie Henningsen (1996) stated that research recommended that students undertake meaningful tasks that are truly problematic. Finally, Elizabeth City and colleagues (2009) presented the fifth principle of the instructional core: "The real accountability system is in the tasks that students are asked to do" (p. 31). To create quality mathematics curriculum for algebra, we would begin each unit of study with a challenging mathematical task, one that researchers called "cognitively demanding," or "high level" (Stein, Smith, Henningsen, & Silver, 2009).

The second extensively researched strategy was that of students learning in a social context (National Research Council, 2000). Timothy Jones (2009) stated, "Traditional instruction in the public schools has been historically teacher driven" (p. 144). However, intelligence had been interpreted, in part, as social practice (Resnick & Nelson-Le Gall, 1997). Erik de Corte (2010) addressed the role of the learning situation as participatory and social, and he addressed the collaborative nature of learning. Finally, Christina Hinton and Kurt Fischer (2010) stated, "Children and adolescents learn in a social context, and the human brain is primed for social interaction" (p. 126). Thus, the learning, built around the tasks in Apollo, would be student centered and teacher facilitated.

ORGANIZING THE WRITING TEAM

We organized the team in what we saw as the most efficient way for writing and producing the curriculum, but that proved to be much more difficult than we had thought. Before 2008, the high school instructional coaches had been divided into groups of three to four, by high school subject—Algebra I, geometry, Algebra II, and precalculus—to write curriculum based on our adopted textbook. That curriculum consisted of (a) a time line, (b) activities for presenting concepts, (c) suggestions for assessment, and (d) resources for reteaching, all of which were textbook aligned. In order to write a brain-based curriculum, we began by assigning everyone to Algebra I, and we divided them into areas of responsibility:

design, research, implementation, integration, cognitively demanding (high-level) task creation, writing, assessment, and publishing. We soon discovered that timing was a constant and insurmountable problem.

Once a task was created, it had to be vetted by the entire team for mathematical correctness, degree of challenge, implementation issues, and methods of assessment. Then it flowed to the writers and publishers. That process held up the research team and task creators, as they waited for a finished product on which to base the next unit. We knew immediately we had the wrong structure, and the project manager wisely suggested that we assign each team a particular algebra topic, or concept, to develop entirely. We reorganized the coaches into four four-person teams, and each team was responsible for every part of a complete unit. They researched and developed high-level tasks; created connective lessons based on the task concepts; provided the teachers with detailed descriptions of the class activities, including directions for utilizing the lesson's technology; developed and wrote assessments, both formative and summative that included ample practice of items aligned to state assessments; and prepared the entire unit for publishing.

FACILITATING THE TEACHER

We tried to think of everything a teacher would need to implement reformed algebra curriculum in a whole new way. The curriculum, with a suggested pacing calendar, was loaded onto our district's website, and we put it on pin drives for teachers as well. When it was appropriate to provide content to students via direct instruction, colorful, engaging, and often interactive PowerPoint presentations were a click away. Teachers could also utilize lessons for interactive whiteboards. We created detailed "Teacher Notes" for each of the high-level tasks and included them in the curriculum. The notes explained not only what to do but also the evidence-based reasons for doing it. They also included scaffolded questions that the teacher could ask the students as they worked on the tasks to facilitate conceptual understanding, and they listed possible misconceptions students might have as well. To keep close contact with the teachers, we scheduled informal after-school meetings once a week at different campuses to just get together with teachers and talk about what was going well, what wasn't, and what we could do to improve. We were all available at any time by phone or via email, and we visited the teacher in person any time we were asked. Of course, for many of the schools, having an instructional coach on campus was an enormous help.

Homework was built into the curriculum that was often based on the classroom tasks. Sometimes a similar task or an extension of the concept was copied by the teachers and distributed to students to be worked at home. However, we thought that parents might be concerned about the lack of a textbook, and I asked my high school supervisors to create a parent website on the district server. We began to place the concept development PowerPoints on the website, and we even narrated them in English and Spanish. A parent or tutor, or the student, could access the site and, with a click, watch the conceptual development of the mathematical topic while listening to the narration. I thought that not having a textbook resource for every lesson would present a problem for parents, but I never received one complaint.

DAY-TO-DAY CURRICULUM DEVELOPMENT

Fridays were often a whirlwind of activity, trying to do in eight hours what would normally take two to three days to accomplish. Generally, we used most of Friday mornings and early afternoons for writing, and we often gathered as a group late on Friday afternoons to review and vet each unit. Reviewing and getting feedback from the entire team accomplished two extremely important considerations. First, every coach (a former classroom teacher with excellent student achievement results) on the entire team heard all the mathematical thinking that went into the creation of each unit, and the discussions that occurred during review provided excellent reflection on the best methodology for implementing the lesson. Secondly, since everyone was intricately involved in finalizing each unit, each coach became a top-notch facilitator for his or her teachers during implementation back at their campuses. The mathematics department team had the highest level of expertise in the district curriculum, complete with the most current instructional technology. The instructional coaches scheduled and delivered professional development for the teachers in implementing the curriculum, including all the high-level tasks, and they were always well prepared to demonstrate and assist with the use of manipulatives and technology.

We planned and scheduled a late spring kickoff for Apollo in May for Algebra I teachers, administrators, and the Learning Community leaders. The algebra teachers had been involved with us in district professional development for nearly three years, reading and learning the research as well, and many were familiar with the Principles of Learning. What they did not have was a coherent curriculum that they could follow with all the principles embedded in it. Of approximately 120 algebra teachers, about 65 attended the meeting, and our supportive Learning Community administrator made an inspiring speech endorsing our new direction, stating his conviction that Apollo, built on extensive research, would enhance student achievement in Algebra I. Within days, schools closed, and the end of the school year gave us more time to use every day for creating curriculum. Our efforts really intensified in the summer, and we worked long, hard days. Sometimes tempers flared, and we had to hash out the best solution to a problem. A few times we just tabled an issue for a couple of days. Other times, we were so enamored with the project that we had to be told to leave the building so it could be locked for the evening.

THE BRAIN AHA!

That summer, the journey was becoming more complex for me personally as I was learning more about what brain-based strategies really meant, which suggested another layer to the new curriculum. In the early 2000s, I had sent a team of elementary supervisors to conferences conducted by Eric Jensen, author of *Brain-Based Learning* (1995). The elementary coordinator returned with such a wealth of material that she presented extensive professional development on brain-based strategies that would enhance learning. I was hearing something I knew instinctively to be true. As a classroom teacher, I had used strategies, including the use of manipulatives, whenever appropriate to help students understand the "why" behind the math concepts, but I had never heard them described as brain based. Then, when the district began collaborating with the University of Pittsburgh, I was so enthralled with studying the research that I enrolled in Texas A&M University, Commerce, to deepen my knowledge. As we were writing curriculum in the summer of 2008, I was taking a doctoral course titled "Creating Brain-Based Schools." It was as if the idea of learning strategies based on brain research had come full circle for me.

The professor of that course, Dr. Timothy B. Jones, talked about long-term memory and how brain research was pointing toward pedagogy that facilitated conceptual development. The more he talked, the more I connected what he was saying with what I had learned from the IFL. He taught that the brain is naturally curious, and the IFL said that students should be given interesting tasks to work on in class rather than being given information. He taught that the brain is naturally social, and the IFL said students should engage in Principles of Learning characterized by collaboration, such as "socialized intelligence"™ and "accountable talk"™ in the classroom (University of Pittsburgh, 2005). Furthermore, Dr. Jones taught that learning is experiential and that the brain searches for meaning, and the IFL stated that students should be given meaningful and challenging problems on which to work. In other words, the work of cognitive scientists, university researchers and educators, and neurobiologists and brain-learning theorists were intertwined in a way that added significant value to the idea that we could richly enhance learning for students.

In addition, as we studied *The Brain, Education and the Competitive Edge* (Caine & Caine, 2001), I came to understand the importance of experience. Similar to their assertions in chapter 3 in this book, Caine and Caine explained, "Experience of is not the same as knowing about" (p. 57). That was it! That was what was missing from the Apollo algebra curriculum. Some of the high-level tasks, in fact as many as possible, had to be experienced by our students!

As an example, we had adapted a great task from TEXTEAMS, the University of Texas at Austin Dana Center's Algebra I: 2000 and Beyond resources for Texas school districts. It was called "Bathing the Dog." Students were given a scenario about bathing a dog that included filling the tub, going to get the dog and placing him in the tub, and bathing him. The dog tries to get out, but he is put back in the tub, and after bathing him and taking him out, the tub is drained. The task addresses the relationship between the water level and the time spent bathing the dog. Students are asked to do the following:

1. Write a description of the changes in the water level as you proceed.
2. Make a graph of the water level in the tub over the time period of the bathing process, labeling each change on the graph.

3. Tell how the graph would change if the sides of the tub were graduated so that they widened from bottom to top.
4. Tell how the graph would change if your dog liked taking a bath and didn't move while you bathed him.
5. Make a poster to present to the class that describes bathing the dog.

I realized that the only thing the problem lacked was a brain-based strategy context; thus, we needed to make it experiential, not experimental (big difference)! The project manager was on summer vacation, but a couple of the elementary specialists were in the office, so I explained my idea to them, that we had to "dunk a dog" to make the task brain based. Of course, they had been to the Jensen workshops, so it made perfect sense to them, and they were more than willing to help. In a catalog, the elementary supervisors found a six-inch-tall, clear, plastic cylindrical tub with a seven-inch diameter. It would make a perfect doggie bathtub, and we could use markers for measuring water levels. Then I asked them to find a relatively small object that would simulate the dog. The coordinator, an expert in brain-learning strategies, made a great suggestion. She said that students should be told what they were going to do the next day in class, and then they should be asked to bring something from home to use as their dog. What a great brain-based idea! That made the task personal, and the students would love using what they brought from home, whether they actually had a dog or not. Some students painted dog faces on their objects (for some, cans of soup), and of course, they named their dogs as well. One of the forward-thinking teachers at the district's all-girls school assigned the problem to her students to do at home. Their presentations were amazing! Several groups of girls made posters with rich descriptions of the bathing process, tables of data, and graphs of water levels over time with explanations, and many included catchy titles and pictures of their very own dogs taking a bath.

HANDS-ON ALGEBRA

Since we included experiential tasks as much as possible, I used much of the math budget that year to launch Apollo, which meant that I bought for each algebra teacher items such as remote control cars (feet per minute in the hallway could translate to miles per hour, or we could race several cars and measure distances traveled, stopping distances, etc.; for that order, I had to write an "official" explanation of what I was going to do with all those cars!). In addition, I bought weight gauges, motion detectors, light probes, force sensors, and manipulatives of all kinds. I bought paper cups, rubber bands, marbles, rulers, poster paper, and markers. I bought Texas Instruments Nspire™ calculators so each student had one to use in class. I was aware, we all were aware, that implementation was crucial. We made absolutely sure that teachers had all of the curriculum, in a format that could easily be presented on a Smart Board™ if they wanted, and all the "stuff" necessary, so that students could explore, hypothesize, conjecture, reason, discuss, write, graph, present, demonstrate, and explain. In short, they could use mathematics to solve problems and have the same experiences in their learning that mathematicians have in theirs!

LAUNCHING APOLLO

In August, at the end of the week when teachers typically returned to prepare for the coming school year, I asked principals to allow Algebra I teachers to attend a one-day math department technology fair. We reserved several rooms in our professional development building, and teachers could visit as many as they wanted and ask as many questions as they had. We were ready to show them every lesson for the first six weeks of school and how to implement each and every piece of technology that was involved. In addition, we carefully reviewed each curriculum guide to make sure all the instructional considerations made sense and was easy to use. Each hour, a new session began on setting up and using classroom technology or on the first six weeks of curriculum and how to read it and use it. It was a fun day and very profitable. Teachers left assured that they could implement the curriculum, and they were excited about welcoming students on Monday morning. We were excited, too, and the supervisors and instructional coaches (who had created the curriculum, including the cognitively demanding tasks) would be on campuses Monday morning to help as well.

Our curriculum for the first six weeks included a problem in which students used a motion detector connected to a computer and a calculator.

I asked the coaches to move the problem to the first day or two of school. I wanted our students to experience fun, rather than fear, as they entered high school algebra for the first time. Here is how it worked: A student would view a graph projected on a screen and then attempt to replicate the same graph by walking to and away from the motion detector. The student's classmates couldn't help shouting for him or her to move one way or another or to slow down or speed up. It gave students immediate, meaningful knowledge of what a graph is, how it may be formed, and how it may be changed. They loved it.

In addition, we began to receive feedback from teachers. One teacher said that she always knew this was the way kids learned, but she just didn't have the time and resources to create the curriculum. Other emails included the following comments:

- What an excellent way to start off the first couple of days of school. —K. Bentley
- Finally, a voice has been heard regarding teaching techniques used in China, Japan, Singapore, and so forth. How soon can such be implemented in lower grades? [Although] challenging . . . I am seeing more of them respond. —A. Richmond
- We had an open house for parents last week, and I set up the walking graphs . . . students couldn't wait to show their parents—and have them walk the graphs. —C. Wingard
- I think that the curriculum that you and your team are creating should quickly become a great resource for the nation's math classes, especially the urban districts (but, really, any district). The lessons are high interest, clear visually, and should lead to a deep understanding of the topic for our wide range of learners. —J. Hill

Several teachers reported student comments such as, "Are you sure this is a math class? This is too much fun to be algebra." Another student saw the motion-detector activity and asked the teacher why they didn't do "stuff" like that last year when he was in her class. At some schools, a lot of excitement was caused when principals stopped in the algebra classes and walked the graphs with the students. We were very gratified to receive teachers' emails, comments, and notes about all the positive student responses to the new experiential algebra curriculum.

ONGOING PROFESSIONAL DEVELOPMENT

Since we were creating a disciplinary, literacy/brain-based curriculum as the year progressed, it was necessary to meet with all the algebra teachers, in groups of thirty, near the end of each six-week grading period in all-day pullout sessions. During those days, we would walk through the curriculum for the next six weeks, and we would all do the high-level tasks together. That was a fun, relaxed day of teacher-coach learning for everyone. Of course, we had some principals who expressed concern about the teachers being away from their students for one day, but many recognized the benefit to students for teachers to experience what their students were going to experience. Teachers had an opportunity to bring up misconceptions that students might have, and often, they added to the questions involved in the tasks, making them even richer.

There were also some very forward-thinking principals who came and spent time with their teachers, working the tasks with them. They walked motion detectors, and they got on the floor to measure heights of weighted paper cups as marbles were added or subtracted. They contributed to the data-collection charts and the discussions around the questions that were part of the problems, and they helped prepare the presentation posters about the mathematics involved in the tasks. Best of all, at the end of the day, the teachers were well prepared, and they took back cognitively demanding tasks, and the curriculum built around them, to their students. They reported back to us how much the students were enjoying algebra, and that made all of the work so worthwhile.

FEEDBACK AND RESULTS

As fall progressed, we continued to write fast and furiously. Fridays always began with coach reports on what was happening in the classrooms, which parts of the curriculum were hugely successful, and where we could improve for next year. Many teachers continued to report student engagement in algebra like never before, and we began to think about student achievement. Dallas ISD administered an Assessment of Course Performance (ACP), a final exam at the end of the fall and spring semesters for core courses. At the end of the 2008 fall semester, we were cautiously optimistic about the ACP results for Algebra I. When the results were posted, we examined Algebra I data for the twenty-two comprehensive high schools that were served by coaches, and we found that nineteen of them reported an increase in the percent of correct responses from the Algebra I ACP of the previous year. Twelve of the schools had an increase of five or more percentage points, and three of the schools had an increase of ten or more points! We felt like shouting, but we didn't celebrate too loudly because the much more significant state assessment was still months away.

In the spring semester, usually in mid to late April, school districts in Texas administered the TAKS. The results were made available by the end of May so that students who needed remedial help could do so in summer months. Early one evening in late May, probably just after five o'clock, most of the instructional coaches had left for home. I was in my office preparing for summer professional development, when the Apollo project manager walked in and informed me that the district results for the grade nine TAKS were available. Anxiously, I asked him to print them from the TEA website so we could take a look.

We expected gains because our curriculum was based on the best current research, but we were not naive. In a district of approximately 160,000 students, there were surely many Algebra I teachers who closed their doors and taught math in the exact way they were taught, using the textbook as the curriculum. The coaches provided ongoing feedback regarding which teachers were following the brain-compatible, experiential curriculum and those who gave it lukewarm lip service but didn't implement the tasks appropriately.

The gains were incredible! We expected to do well, but we thought something must be wrong. When a district has significant gains on a state test, it is never time to celebrate until the overall state data have been published. After all, if we gained ten points and the state gained twelve, we actually fared poorly. But we gained at rates above those of the state . . . for every student group! And our Hispanic scores actually topped the state's performance by eight points! We decided to see if we were missing something or if this could be the actual results. I in my office, and he in his, we recalculated the gains separately. I actually used paper and pencil and a four-function calculator to calculate Dallas's scores from three years past, and then I compared them to the same scores for the entire state. I think I was still astonished that the gains were so remarkable.

Chapter Six

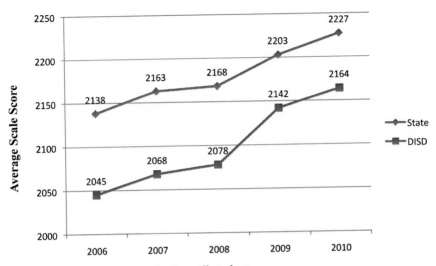

Figure 6.1. **Mathematics grade nine: All students.**

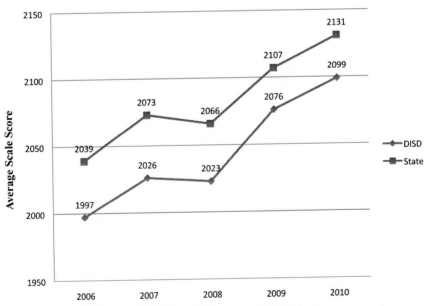

Figure 6.2. **Mathematics grade nine: African American students.**

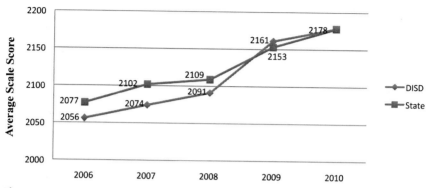

Figure 6.3. **Mathematics grade nine: Hispanic students.**

From 2008 to 2009, the average scale score on the mathematics TAKS for all grade nine students across Texas increased by thirty-five points, from 2,168 to 2,203. For the same year, the average scale score in mathematics TAKS for all grade nine students in Dallas ISD increased by sixty-four points, from 2,078 to 2,142. The gap between the grade nine mathematics scores of all students in Dallas ISD, an urban school district, and the state closed by twenty-nine points in one school year. African American students in Dallas ISD also had a more significant increase in the grade nine mathematics average scale score of fifty-three points from 2008 to 2009 than African American students across the state who gained forty-one points. Finally, the increase in average scale scores on the math TAKS of Hispanic students across the state was forty-four points. The increase for Hispanic students in Dallas ISD was seventy points, and in fact, the Dallas Hispanic students' average scale score surpassed that of the state by eight points.

THE AFTERMATH

So, what happened afterward? Principals asked us to create the same kind of curriculum for geometry and for grade eight, and we did. But the celebration we were having over the success of our students wasn't district-wide. We had critics, those who did not know mathematics content or instruction and whose motives could be questioned, but we had great support from those who understood the importance of the gains our students had made. Douglas McLeod (2003) addressed the difficulty that NCTM leaders had in explaining reform ideas to the public and to teachers. The difficulty certainly persists today. Communication, ongoing and two way, with all stakeholders, teachers, administrators, and the public, is critical to successful implementation of a brain-enriched curriculum.

Some algebra teachers said they would never, ever return to a typical textbook. A few across the large city had seen students struggle with mathematics and finally achieve success in solving challenging problems. They saw the light in their eyes—and not of turning in all twenty homework problems, or of working a problem "just like you showed me, and I got the right answer." They saw, as we did, students experiencing the joy of real thinking. For all of them and for all of us, there is no going back.

REFERENCES

American Association for the Advancement of Science. (2000). Algebra for all—Not with today's textbooks, says AAAS. Project 2061 press release. Washington, D.C.

Applications Reform in Secondary Education (ARISE; 1998). *Mathematics: Modeling our world, course I* (Annotated teacher's ed.). Cincinnati: South-Western Educational Publishing.

Bruner, J. (1960). *The process of education.* Cambridge, MA: Harvard University Press.

Caine, G., & Caine, R. (2001). *The brain, education and the competitive edge.* New York: Rowman & Littlefield Education.

City, E., Elmore, R., Fiarman, S., & Teital, L. (2009). *Instructional rounds in education.* Cambridge, MA: Harvard Education Press.

Clements, M. A. (2003). An outsider's view of North American school mathematics. In G. Stanic & J. Kilpatrick (Eds.), *A history of school mathematics.* Reston, VA: National Council of Teachers of Mathematics.

de Corte, E. (2010). Historical developments in the understanding of learning. In H. Dumont, D. Istance, & F. Benevides (Eds.), *The nature of learning.* Paris: Organization for Economic Co-operation and Development.

Donoghue, E. F. (2003). Algebra and geometry textbooks in twentieth-century America. In G. Stanic & J. Kilpatrick (Eds.), *A history of school mathematics.* Reston, VA: National Council of Teachers of Mathematics.

Doyle, W., & Carter, K. (1984). Academic tasks in classrooms. *Curriculum Inquiry, 14*(2), 129–149.

Educational Testing Service. (2009). Frequently asked questions about the algebra end-of-course assessment. Retrieved from http://www.ets.org/.

Hinton, C., & Fischer, K. (2010). Learning from the developmental and biological perspective. In H. Dumont, D. Istance, & F. Benevides (Eds.), *The nature of learning*. Paris: Organization for Economic Co-operation and Development.

Institute for Learning. (2009–2012). History. University of Pittsburgh. Retrieved October 2, 2012, from http://ifl.lrdc.pitt.edu/ifl/index.php/about/history.

Institute for Learning. (2006). *A framework for disciplinary literacy in middle and high schools*. Pittsburgh: University of Pittsburgh.

Jensen, E. (1995). *Brain-based learning*. San Diego: Brain Store.

Jones, T. B. (2009). John Dewey: Still ahead of his time. In P. Jenlink (Ed.), *Dewey's democracy and education revisited*. Lanham, MD: Rowman & Littlefield Education.

Kieran, C. (1992). The learning and teaching of school algebra. In D. Grouws (Ed.), *Handbook of research on mathematics teaching and learning*. Reston, VA: National Council of Teachers of Mathematics.

Matthews, M., & Farmer, J. (2008). Factors affecting the Algebra I achievement of academically talented learners (Report). *Journal of Advanced Academics*. Retrieved April 13, 2009, from http://www.accessmylibrary.com/.

McLeod, D. (2003). From consensus to controversy: The story of the NCTM standards. In G. Stanic & J. Kilpatrick (Eds.), *A history of school mathematics*. Reston, VA: National Council of Teachers of Mathematics.

Moses, R. P., & Cobb, C. E., Jr. (2001). *Radical equations: Math literacy and civil rights*. Boston: Beacon.

National Council of Teachers of Mathematics. (1989). *Curriculum and evaluation standards for school mathematics*. Reston, VA: National Council of Teachers of Mathematics.

National Research Council. (2000). How people learn: Brain, mind, experience, and school. In J. D. Bransford, A. L. Brown, & R. R. Cocking (Eds.), *Committee on developments in the science of learning and committee on learning research and educational practice*. Washington, DC: National Academy Press.

RAND Corporation. (2003). *Mathematical proficiency for all students*. Mathematics Study Panel. Santa Monica, CA: RAND Education.

Resnick, L. B. (2003). From aptitude to effort: A new foundation for our schools. *Journal of the American Academy of Arts and Sciences, 124*(4), 55–62.

Resnick, L. B. (1999). Making America smarter. *Education Week, 40*, 38–40. Retrieved November 7, 2012, from http://www.edweek.org/.

Resnick, L. B., & Glennan, T. K., Jr. (2002). Leadership for learning: A theory of action for urban school districts. In A. M. Hightower, M. S. Knapp, J. A. Marsh, & M. W. MacLaughlin (Eds.), *School districts and instructional renewal: Critical issues in educational leadership*. New York: Teachers College Press.

Resnick, L. B., & Nelson-Le Gall, S. (1997). Socializing intelligence. In L. Smith, J. Dockrell, & P. Tomlinson (Eds.), *Piaget, Vygotsky and beyond.* London: Routledge.

Senk, S. L. (1989). Toward algebra in the year 2000 or a reaction to: "School algebra in the year 2000." In S. Wagner & C. Kieran (Eds.), *Research issues in the learning and teaching of algebra.* Reston, VA: National Council of Teachers of Mathematics.

Seymour, D., & Davidson, P. S. (2003). A history of nontextbook material. In G. Stanic & J. Kilpatrick (Eds.), *A history of school mathematics.* Reston, VA: National Council of Teachers of Mathematics.

Stapel, E. (2006–2009). Why do I have to take algebra? Retrieved June 15, 2009, from http://www.purplemath.com/modules/why_math.htm.

Stein, M. K., Grover, B. W., & Henningsen, M. (1996). Building student capacity for mathematical thinking and reasoning: An analysis of mathematical tasks used in reform classrooms. *American Educational Research Journal, 33,* 455–488.

Stein, M. K., Smith, M. S., Henningsen, M. A., & Silver, E. A. (2009). *Implementing standards-based mathematics instruction: A casebook for professional development* (2nd ed.). New York: Teachers College Press.

University of Pittsburgh. (2005). *Principles of learning for effort-based education.* Pittsburgh: University of Pittsburgh.

U.S. Department of Education. (1997, October 20). Mathematics equals opportunity (White paper). Washington, D.C.

Vygotsky, L. (1978). *Mind in society.* Cambridge, MA: Harvard University Press.

Willis, J. (2006). *Research-based strategies to ignite student learning.* Alexander, VA: Association for Supervision and Curriculum Development.

Part III

THE ROAD MAP

Planning and Implementing the Work Ahead

In the final part, a cohesive road map is presented for changing the paradigm and culture in any school setting to a brain-compatible and natural learning environment. In chapter 7, the critical elements for developing a Professional Learning Community (PLC) will be outlined. The PLC will be the vehicle to begin an effective transformation of school culture from traditional teaching pedagogy to brain-compatible, natural learning pedagogy in an organizationally healthy, safe, and respectful manner. Chapter 8 will introduce our unique "Cogito for Innovative Schools" model that will create a process and structure for developing and implementing short- and long-range plans, within the PLC, to ensure successful implementation.

Educators can have all the knowledge and skill to lead and never actually do it. Chapter 9 was written to deal with that phenomenon . . . having the courage to do what you know needs to be done and to succeed in doing it. Finally, chapter 10 includes final thoughts on the journey that is this book. Voices from administrators and teachers will be shared, and some parting thoughts representing all of the collective wisdom of the authors will be presented.

At the conclusion of part III, "The Road Map," the following beliefs and paradigms will resonate:

* We believe that brain-compatible, natural learning is as applicable to changing the practice of educators as it is to changing the way learning occurs for students.

- We believe that the Professional Learning Community (PLC) is a natural process of learning and change for everyone in the school or district organization.
- We believe that leaders must have courage, regardless of position, to facilitate innovative change and improvement in their school organization.
- We believe that anyone reading this book has the abilities and courage to make brain-compatible, natural learning happen!

Chapter Seven

The Brain and
the Learning Community

Lawrence Kohn

By building an effective and healthy learning community, a school can substantially reduce stress felt by those who work and learn within it, and they can therefore function more effectively—and get better results. In any community, a key factor is relationships and how they are formed. Some ways of being together facilitate a process, but others impede it. People need to listen to and respect each other, even if they have major differences of opinion and varying goals. They need to feel safe in a group to express and test opinions and to agree to disagree. And they need to be able to respect the overall process and be able to handle issues that persist over time and vary in degree of difficulty. All this means that any effective and stable learning community needs to have some accepted protocols for talking and behaving, and an atmosphere conducive to effective functioning.

—Geoffrey Caine and Renate Caine (2010)

This description of an effective and healthy learning community stresses a context of safety, relationships, and respect. These contextual factors are derived from Caine and Caine's seminal work in 1990, in which they transformed the theoretical foundations of brain-based learning into a set of twelve Brain/Mind Learning Principles (see chapter 3; Caine & Caine 2010, 2011):

1. All learning engages the physiology.
2. The brain/mind is social.
3. The search for meaning is innate.
4. The search for meaning occurs through patterning.

5. Emotions are critical to patterning.
6. The brain/mind processes parts and wholes simultaneously.
7. Learning involves both focused attention and peripheral perception.
8. Learning is both conscious and unconscious.
9. There are at least two approaches to memory.
10. Learning is developmental.
11. Complex learning is enhanced by challenge and inhibited by threat associated with helplessness or fatigue.
12. Each brain is uniquely organized.

By default, all twelve principles relate to the process of creating, implementing, and sustaining a healthy and effective learning community. That said, this process does not happen simply by opening a new school with new teachers and leadership, nor does it happen when a principal takes over an existing school. While research and methods for creating a learning community are widely available, it takes the collective efforts of the principal and the teachers in a school to work through the process of birthing and sustaining a healthy learning community.

This chapter serves to help school leaders design, implement, and sustain a brain-enriched environment in a school through the natural and intentional changes that occur through a learning community. Relationships will be drawn between Caine and Caine's twelve principles and the structures and processes of a highly effective learning community. How leaders' roles and actions create the conditions for such communities to exist will also be discussed. References to the twelve principles will occur throughout the chapter.

PROFESSIONAL LEARNING COMMUNITY: HISTORY AND NEED

For the duration of this chapter, learning community will be referred to as "Professional Learning Community" (PLC), as this is the term most often ascribed to the structures and processes of learning communities involved in an education setting. PLCs in schools occur when an entire faculty regularly meets with a focus on essential and shared issues regardless of the content they teach; this entails educators taking collective responsibility for accomplishing a mutual purpose for the school and collaborating to reach this purpose. In essence, a PLC has a shared vision. How did the concept of PLC develop, how does this relate to brain-enriched learning, and why is it so essential to create the related conditions of PLC in schools?

The historical development of this concept may have begun in 1967 with an article published by researcher and professor Fred Newmann titled "Education and Community." The article presents an argument for modern schools and formal education to develop a broader sense of community rather than the fragmented sense of community seen in most public schools. The authors also articulated that the alternative movement in the late 1960s and early 1970s was an attempt to restore a sense of community in the schools. Two movement paradigms of community existed in this time period: (1) a movement within school communities that comprised like-minded individuals who cared about one and other, and (2) a movement to break down the school walls and connect students with their community.

It is important to note that although brain-enriched learning research and practices were not in play during this time, the very organic nature of brain-enriched learning can be sensed in the first movement, where an emphasis on social learning, patterning, and emotions were already being considered in schools. Following this, researchers began to look at the difference between public schools and private schools. One key finding of this work was that there was a much stronger sense of collective responsibility and purpose in the private schools. It was this sense of community that the researchers identified as one reason for the private schools' slightly greater success. Newmann commissioned researcher Tony Bryk to do the first quantitative analysis of communal school organizations on student achievement in 1988.

Bryk studied high schools and created scales of communal measures such as the degree of respect staff members had for each other and the extent to which they shared goals. He concluded that the higher degree of communal organization that occurred in the high schools, the higher the levels of student achievement. Once again, one of Caine and Caine's principles (principle 11) is reflected in these findings: communal organizations decrease threat and increase respect and a sense of belonging. Contrasts were made with more bureaucratic-type schools that had strict divisions of labor and were more rules based. This led to more studies on bureaucratic versus communal organizations. Within this, more careful analysis of teachers occurred. Specifically, the question was raised, "What is the difference between community in general and a professional community?" From this, the definition of community, which originally included the notion of shared goals, was expanded to include shared goals for student learning. This has evolved into the current terminology, the PLC.

PLCs have specific conditions, structures, and processes that foster brain-enriched learning. These conditions, processes, and structures are considered parts of a system that rely on each other and should not be seen as independent entities. It is this organic and living system that Caine and Caine (2010) refer to when they assert that relationships, respect, safety, and collaboration must be central to a healthy PLC. Largely based on the work of Newmann (1996), these conditions and processes are found in healthy PLCs.

Shared Norms and Values

The first condition is shared norms and values. Where a PLC thrives, shared values are found in school practices. For example, teachers assume that all students can learn, despite the many impediments they may face outside of school. Extra efforts are made in order to ensure that students also learn in after-school activities. Members of a learning community display in both action and deed their shared beliefs and values about education, their roles, interpersonal and intrapersonal issues, and the school's role in relationship to the community.

Collective Focus

Aside from shared norms and values, an effective PLC must have a collective focus on student learning. Faculties discuss and act on opportunities to improve students' learning and enhance achievement. This goes beyond simply focusing on activities or techniques simply to get students' attention. Teachers discuss methods in which their actions promote students' intellectual development.

Reflective Dialogue

In addition, an effective PLC sees teachers engage in reflective dialogue. Reflective dialogue intensifies teachers' mindfulness of their teaching methods and their outcomes. In a strong PLC, teachers use group activities to reflect, discuss, and then evaluate themselves and their schools. These critiques can address various issues such as the selection of subject matter and strategies for presentation, assessing student learning, and the social conditions of school.

Publicize Their Practice

Teachers in highly functioning PLCs publicize their practice. Publicizing practice is the analysis and evaluation of teacher effectiveness in teaching students to construct their knowledge skillfully. To do so, teachers must come up with ways of interacting with students that are not well defined in textbooks or in professional literature. Teachers cannot do this on an individual basis. Peers become a critical source of insight and feedback. Teachers learn new ways to talk about what they do by sharing doubts about practice and at the same time create new relationships that help advance their work. The notion of shutting the door and teaching in anonymity disappears in an effective PLC.

Collaboration

Furthermore, collaboration is a necessary and consistent activity in an effective PLC. Collaboration can be viewed as an outcome of engaging in reflective dialogue and publicizing practice. When teachers collaborate productively, they engage in reflective dialogue and they watch and react to each other's teaching, curriculum, and assessment practices. They engage in collective planning of curriculum, assessment, and instruction in the pursuit of challenging students to think critically and intellectually. They respectfully debate and discuss the conditions that make learning engaging and relevant for students. Collaboration is the core of a successful PLC.

Effective Leadership

Finally, effective leadership is the underpinning support in successful PLCs, and successful leaders in PLCs have distinct characteristics. First, leaders take on new roles in order to work with teachers to increase learning and achievement in the school. They delegate authority, develop collaborative decision-making processes, and step back from being the main problem solver, turning instead to their PLCs for critical decisions. Leaders in a PLC define themselves as at the center of the school's staff rather than at the top. They also work effectively to stimulate professional discussion and to create networks of conversation that tie faculty together around common issues of instruction and teaching (Newmann, 1996). Clearly, the actions of effective leaders correlate to Caine and Caine's twelve principals, as the focus of an effective leader in a PLC is to build relationships, create a culture of safety and respect for faculty and students, and to negate any feelings of threat.

While all of this sounds appealing, there are even more important reasons to create PLCs and thus develop effective leaders who understand the brain-enriched principles that relate to the conditions and processes of PLCs. Perhaps most important is the current condition of public education in the United States. Educators, policy makers, and the general public continue to demand schools that create students who can think critically, problem solve, collaborate, and function in teams. However, the current system in place produces a 71.7 percent graduation rate, and of students who persist and continue to higher education, over 40 percent are slotted into remedial courses (Conley, 2007; EPE Research Center, 2011). When disaggregated further, African Americans and Hispanic students face a graver reality, as only 58 percent of these students graduate from high school. This translates to 1.2 million students dropping out, nearly 6,400 per day, or one every twenty-seven seconds (EPE Research Center, 2011).

The social, moral, and economic effects cannot be discounted, in particular as a global economy puts additional pressure on this nation to produce citizens who are intellectually and socially prepared at an optimal level. Reform efforts abound: small schools, class size adjustments, the use of high-yield instructional strategies, personalized learning, No Child Left Behind, and most recently a call for a core national curriculum. However, research shows that effective PLCs, in particular those in which brain-enriched learning experiences are pervasive, may reverse these trends (Hord & Sommers, 2008). Such schools have higher student and faculty attendance; students at these schools achieve at higher rates, and they feel safer and more respected (Huffman & Hipp, 2003). Perhaps most important, leaders in PLCs must play specific roles and engage in specific initiatives to create brain-enriched and effective PLCs in order to improve the data shared above.

THEORETICAL FRAMEWORK: HOW LEADERS CREATE BRAIN-ENRICHED CONDITIONS IN PLCS

There is a theoretical framework for creating, implementing, and sustaining an effective brain-enriched PLC in a school. This framework is born from personal leadership experiences in a school where a highly effective PLC was created and sustained. In this framework, effective leadership (the catalyst) builds trust (an outcome) between the leader and the staff. As trust heightens between the staff and the leader, staff relational trust (an outcome) heightens, partly due to the roles the leader played and partly due to positive behaviors in which the staff engages (collaboration, willingness to continuously learn and improve, being accountable, and being enculturated). If left unscathed, these trust features and the positive behaviors lead to the "regulating ideal," a collective focus on student learning and achievement (Kohn, 2001).

On the other hand, lack of self-efficacy, lack of cultural knowledge, and personality pathologies deter a heightened level of trust and therefore are detrimental to an effective PLC. These positive and negative influences create a dynamic situation where trust is in a continuous flux; influences by either the staff or effective leadership can return the trust, but these negative influences will potentially exist in some fashion. This dynamic situation in turn affects the continuum of collectivity the staff can reach toward for a pure focus on student learning and achievement. Because of the dynamics depicted in this theoretical framework, a pure collective focus on student learning and achievement as a regulating ideal cannot be fully established. Overall, the effective PLC always strives for this ideal, but the central dynamics of this model, in conjunction with the efforts to reach the regulating ideal, place the professional community along the continuum of collectivity, always affected by positive and negative influences. How this theoretical framework works in action reveals what leaders and teachers do to create an effective brain-enriched PLC (Kohn, 2001).

EFFECTIVE LEADERSHIP ROLES

Whether starting a school or entering an existing school, a leader needs to play essential roles to create the conditions for an effective brain-enriched PLC. In these roles, the leader may be seen as a catalyst. The first role is the "mirror holder." An effective leader will not simply tell a faculty how they are successful and how they struggle. Instead, he "holds up the mirror" to the faculty and asks two essential questions: Who are we? And, how good are we at who we are? The answer to these questions helps a faculty define or redefine its mission, be reflective about its collective actions, and determine the impact that it has on school culture and student learning and achievement.

To answer these questions, the leader must enact a second role, the "gatherer/synthesizer." The faculty needs to have every bit of information about what is done each day in the school. For example, what collaborative structures exist and why? What decisions are made and how? The leader organizes these data and puts them in a useable form for the staff to analyze. Simply gathering data is not enough; the leader must synthesize them and then allow the faculty to have these data to make informed, shared decisions.

Finally, a leader must be a human potential builder. Leaders should anticipate individual and organizational needs, and provide the training and time to meet those needs. As a leader builds capacity and human potential, a stronger, healthier organizational capacity ensues. From a brain-enriched perspective, attending to the individual needs of a faculty develops a sense of trust and helps improve the self-efficacy of members. Each role correlates to the principles of brain-enriched learning, as each focuses on the human condition within the PLC. Holding up the mirror allows for faculty members to engage in self-analysis and reflection in order to learn and grow as a learning organization. Being handed specific data about their collective actions and decisions provides a context for self-renewal and maintenance. Finally, fostering human potential is at the heart of brain-enriched learning; when leaders provide opportunities for shared leadership and time and opportunity to develop a sense of comfort and self-efficacy for a faculty, the conditions for optimized learning are met. The remainder of this section will be devoted to giving specific examples of actions leaders take within these roles to create and foster a brain-enriched PLC.

Collaboration is the essential action that occurs in a healthy PLC. As such, leaders can leverage collaborative structures and processes to help a faculty learn more about itself, improve individual and collective practice, and improve school culture and climate. For example, the principal can lead the faculty with an ongoing analysis of critical documents, structures, and processes. Below is a list that may apply to some learning organizations; others may have unique structures. Together, they provide a framework for self-analysis and can be given to the faculty as a booklet containing critical documents for such analysis. This allows the faculty to do the following:

- Analyze a synthesis of the goals and activities of the school's improvement plan (SIP), focusing on what the faculty said they would do.
- Analyze a listing of all the collaborative structures in which they could accomplish goals of the SIP, focusing on what the faculty does.
- Analyze each teacher's professional development objectives for the school year. This represents what each staff member individually said she or he would do. These objectives can then be matched with actual staff development that each teacher attended, focusing on what individuals did.
- Analyze the purpose and connection of the designated campus professional development days.
- Analyze efforts by the site-based decision-making team, focusing on how they align with the SIP.
- Analyze the efforts of faculty meetings. Actions the faculty took should be highlighted from minutes of all these meetings.
- Analyze efforts of all other collaborative structures in the same fashion as faculty meetings. This can include department meetings, team meetings, and content-area meetings.
- Analyze any external grant plan's goals, objectives, and activities, focusing on connections or disconnections from the SIP.

The principal can design, create, and teach the faculty how to use a booklet with such information, thus allowing them to discover "how good they are at who they are." This is an extremely important paradigm shift for most learning organizations. Since overidealized views concerning teacher empowerment can be found in most restructuring efforts, conflicts about implementation can overtake restructuring efforts and result in bogged-down efforts. Instead of learning how to be more effective, too much energy is applied to implementation of reforms and burnout can occur, thus decreasing sought-after brain-enriched context.

While faculties typically look at reflections of their actions via surveys and other data, few are presented with such a comprehensive look at themselves. This activity begins the transformation from a typical faculty to a true Professional Learning Community because now the focus of professional inquiry is on themselves, not external resources, research, literature, or the tenets of an external partner. This strongly relates to the notions of self-organization, self-maintaining, self-renewing, and self-transcending in the literature surrounding systems theory and the explanation of how a learning organization learns and improves itself for the purpose of increasing student learning and achievement (Jones, 2013). When faculties engage in this level of self-analysis, opportunities arise to create a healthier and more effective PLC because nearly all twelve principles of brain-enriched learning occur during this process.

Finally, the principal should share leadership and find ways to involve all members of the PLC, not the select few who often take the lead. One method is to set up a rotation of allowing teachers to chair the committees and collaborative structures that run the school. Teachers commit to serving on a combination of the most and least time- and energy-intensive structures in the PLC, thus creating an equitable system where everyone shares in equal efforts to run the school. Most important, each committee or collaborative structure needs norms to ensure the meetings are run smoothly and that each has an outcome statement to ensure the work of the committee stays focused. For example, here are four collaborative structures that might be seen in a PLC and their outcome statements:

- Faculty meetings: Improved internal communication and decision making
- Faculty-advisory meetings: Creation of an advisory curriculum that supports the SIP, creates cohesive advisory units, and builds accountability measures for staff
- Curriculum and instruction planning: Measurable and observable improvement in instruction and assessment practices
- Curriculum and instruction debriefing: Evidence of use of varied instruction and assessments

Those chairing the meetings begin by reviewing the norms and facilitating the meetings around the outcomes; anything discussed or decided should correlate to the outcome. Furthermore, minutes are created for each structure not only for the benefit of the committees and their work but also to provide evidence for the next time the PLC engages in overall self-analysis. This way, the faculty provides much of its own data.

Each year, faculty members rotate to new committees, and each assumes a new leadership position, thus allowing everyone the opportunity for shared leadership through varying paradigms. The principal is building human potential through shared leadership and simultaneously creating a sense of comfort and self-efficacy for faculty members. One can plainly see the correlation to brain/mind principles in this context; members feel a sense of collective responsibility, and no one is left without a significant role. Learning about the school is ongoing and done without a sense of threat, top-down rhetoric, or compliance. Most important, however, are the powerful outcomes as the result of the principal engaging in these roles and actions.

OUTCOMES

As the catalyst in the PLC, the principal holds up the mirror, teaches the learning organization to self-analyze and make collective decisions, and works to build human potential. When this occurs, several outcomes occur that directly correlate to Brain/Mind Learning Principles, and the most striking outcome is trust. Two kinds of trust develop: teacher trust develops with the leader, and staff relational trust develops and builds among faculty members.

Teacher trust develops with the leader primarily because of the roles the principal has played as catalyst. By remaining in the middle of the PLC and not sitting at the top, the leader is sending some powerful messages to the faculty: I trust you to run this school. I trust you to make collective decisions to improve the school. I trust you to hold each other accountable. A typical school has a principal and multiple assistant principals who routinely make decisions and then share them with the faculty. They might seek input in some ways, but ultimately the administration is deciding how the school will run and who will run it. However, if a leader wants a brain-enriched PLC, actions are taken to ensure the faculty is the primary decision maker. This is the way to create a collective focus on student learning and achievement in a climate of trust between the leader and the faculty.

Staff relational trust develops and builds because all members are working collaboratively in the PLC's structures and making shared decisions. They are working not in isolation inside their classrooms but together. Furthermore, recall that a key aspect of a PLC is that practice is publicized. When staff relational trust builds via the shared leadership positions while working in and among the committees that run the school, members are more willing to collaborate about their instruction. A visitation schedule can be created to allow teachers of differing content areas to watch lessons and give each other feedback. Now conditions exist where members are not only collaborating about the school and how it runs but also collaborating about each other's practices in the classroom. Protocols can be applied to help teachers give each other feedback in safe and trusting ways in critical friends groups (see http://www.nsrfharmony.org/).

Principals, however, must also be watchdogs for the ongoing conditions in a PLC that can limit or diminish trust. As members come and go, lack of cultural knowledge can weaken trust. New members must be taught the history of the school and how it is run, and understand they will be expected to become part of a PLC that engages in the actions described above before they begin to work in the organization. This can be done by veterans of the PLC making new members feel welcome and part of essential structures and processes early on in their tenure. Another condition a principal needs to look for is a lack of self-efficacy in any faculty member. Typically, principals appraise a teacher for the purposes of contract renewal tied to teaching abilities and professional responsibilities. However, the principal in a brain-enriched PLC has to be ever wary of members who feel challenged or inhibited by any sort of perceived threat, directly correlating to principle 11. When observed, the leader must work hard to bring that member back to a sense of safety and trust so learning can be optimized for that member, and for the students of that teacher. Therefore, the role of a leader in a brain-enriched PLC is to care for and about the teachers in the PLC the same way teachers would do so for students in their classrooms.

MATRICULATING PRINCIPLES TO THE CLASSROOM

Once a brain-enriched PLC is structured and is self-analytical as described, it can turn its focus from itself and toward the structures and processes that will create brain-enriched classrooms. While this may be achieved in many ways, two of the most effective ways is to create a person-centered classroom management system for the school and to focus on classroom formative assessment inside each classroom. This section will focus on how leaders can implement these efforts to increase student learning and achievement and how each fosters a sense of trust, safety, and self-efficacy for students. The two initiatives strongly correlate to the twelve principles of brain/mind learning.

Person-Centered Classroom Management

The research base relating classroom management and student achievement and a safe and effective classroom environment is indisputable. Margaret Wang, Geneva Haertel, and Herbert Walberg (1993), in a meta-analysis of essential learning behaviors, identified classroom management as being the most important factor that influences student achievement. Furthermore, Robert Marzano's (2003) meta-analysis of over one hundred studies indicates that the quality of student-teacher relationships is the key factor to successful classroom management. Leaders who understand the importance of these findings and use them to help teachers become strong classroom managers will find the dividends to be brain-enriched classrooms.

The paradigm that creates such classrooms is rooted in humanism, particularly in Carl Rogers's work that stems from his person-centered approach as a psychologist, as seen in his book *Freedom to Learn*. The notion of person-centeredness in the classroom translates loosely to creating conditions where the students and teacher work together to create a safe and nurturing environment in the classroom. This is a far departure from the typical behaviorist approach, where the teacher is in sole control of the classroom and students passively comply. The challenge for the leader is to provide the learning and support for teachers to create classrooms where person-centeredness becomes the norm.

The theoretical framework for such classrooms is based on four critical components deeply aligned with the twelve brain/mind principles: prevention, caring, cooperation, and organization. The leader's role is to engrain these components into all classrooms in the school in order to create conditions where learning is optimized. Teachers are taught that prevention of future discipline problems is done early in the school year in a cooperative effort between teachers and students. For example, the teacher may have a few rules to propose to the class to promote a successful learning environment. Students are asked to consider these, discuss them, and then have time to work on their own set of rules with the teacher's help. In the end, a set of rules developed together is fashioned, thus creating the beginning phases of trust, ownership, and cooperation in the classroom.

The teacher must also care for and about all students. This requires listening, reflecting, trusting, and respecting the learner in the classroom. The notion here is to honor the student while honing behavior. Teachers practice listening, reflecting on learning with students, and taking an interest in their lives. They learn over time to meet students where they are in the learning process and to personalize learning as much as possible.

Furthermore, cooperation and organization are at the heart of such classrooms because they lead to ownership, engagement, and greater opportunities for students to learn self-discipline. Trust is an integral part of building cooperation and is built by giving opportunities of ownership of the classroom to the students. Teachers can be taught to delegate the administrative duties of the classroom to students in the form of jobs or positions. Students are taught these roles, and then they engage in them each day. Typical roles are the door manager, paper manager, technology manager, supplies manager, and substitute manager. Dozens more exist. Once delegated into these roles, the students collectively run the classroom, thus feeling empowered and trusted to complete adult tasks. Teachers have more time to focus on instruction, learning, and building relationships with their students.

Classroom managers are made, not born. Certainly, specific personality traits of teachers ease or inhibit the acceptance of creating person-centered classrooms; however, most teachers can be taught how to create them. The leader's role of human potential builder again comes into play as the move to create effective classroom managers of this caliber is ongoing and must become part of the culture of the school. In other words, this does not involve a two-day workshop where teachers then run off and create such classrooms. To create a culture and climate inside classrooms that fosters a sense of safety and trust is ongoing and never stops.

By using the collaborative structures of the school, leaders plan a cycle of learning so teachers already part of the PLC are exposed to ongoing learning concerning person-centered classroom management. For example, faculty meetings cease to be information-sharing sessions and become sessions of learning. Publishing the cycle of learning and sharing it with the PLC shows this to be a focus for the school. Furthermore, teachers new to the PLC can be introduced to this paradigm as they enter the school and are taught the foundational tenets for creating and sustaining such classrooms. While simplistic in nature, the underlying motive is to show the PLC that creating such classrooms is "part of who we are" and not simply the flavor of the day for professional development. Furthermore, once implemented, the actions of the teachers in the PLC have to be closely monitored. Plans are only as good as the paper on which they are written, so what gets paid attention to by the leader is what gets done.

Classroom Formative Assessment

With a safe and caring environment established, learning protocols can be created to ensure brain-enriched classrooms. This is most effectively done through a school-wide focus on classroom formative assessment or assessment for learning. While it seems odd that assessment could be related to brain-enriched learning, it is inextricably linked. Albert Bandura's work on self-efficacy provides this link:

> Perceived self-efficacy is defined as people's beliefs about their capabilities to produce designated levels of performance that exercise influence over events that affect their lives. Self-efficacy beliefs determine how people feel, think, motivate themselves and behave. . . . People's beliefs about their efficacy can be developed by four main sources of influence. The most effective way of creating a strong sense of efficacy is through mastery experiences. Successes build a robust belief in one's personal efficacy. Failures undermine it, especially if failures occur before a sense of efficacy is firmly established. (Bandura, 1994, p. 71)

Mastery experiences build self-efficacy, motivation, and confidence, and classroom formative assessment and its related strategies provide mastery experiences for students.

Assessment, in particular, formative assessment, has a specific working definition that is based on mastery experiences and that builds self-efficacy. The word "assess" comes from the Latin verb *assidere*, meaning "to sit with." During the assessment process, one is supposed to sit with the learner: educators act with and for students; they do not act to them (Green, 1998). However, traditional assessment methods used to prepare teachers mostly result in the use of tests to determine grades and to motivate students to prepare for these assessments. In addition, data from district benchmark tests and state-mandated tests dominate the educational environment in public K–12 schools and supposedly help teachers to make instructional decisions and improve student learning. If the goal is to have students use their minds well and be motivated and engaged learners, schools might lessen their dependence on summative assessments and embrace formative assessments, thus achieving a balanced assessment approach in the classroom.

The working definition in this chapter for formative assessment is "a planned process in which assessment-elicited evidence of students' status is used by teachers to adjust their ongoing instructional procedures or by students to adjust their current learning tactics" (Popham, 2008, p. 6). This definition is synonymous to the term "classroom formative assessment." Classroom formative assessment is not a unit test or a benchmark test but a planned process that involves multiple strategies and techniques. As such, teachers and students use data during the formative assessment process. Teachers change how and what they do to help students master the intended learning, and students change the strategies and ways in which they learn as users of this evidence. The teacher-student adjustments are not made on guesses or on cues but on evidence derived from this planned process (Popham, 2008). It is during this process and through specific strategies and activities that students learn to think critically about the intended learning outcomes and about themselves as learners.

To illustrate a working framework in the classroom, Rick Stiggins and colleagues (2006) and Jan Chappuis (2009) have developed a set of strategies called "Classroom Assessment for Learning"; that is, classroom formative assessment and its associated strategies. These strategies are grouped under three guiding questions that actively engage students in the formative assessment process. The questions provide a guiding structure for students, and the embedded strategies teachers can use are aligned with each question. As is the case with classroom management, principals must lead a detailed and focused approach to helping teachers in the PLC learn how to use these strategies to create brain-enriched learning experiences for students. An explanation of each strategy and how they relate to the brain/mind principles follows.

The first guiding question is, Where am I going? and contains two strategies: (1) provide a clear and understandable vision of the learning target, and (2) use examples and models of strong and weak work. Teachers learn to share the learning targets, expectations, or goals in advance of teaching the lesson, giving the assignment, or doing the activity. Most important, teachers are taught how to use language students understand and to check to make sure students understand the intended learning. While current practice in teacher preparation guides teachers to write objectives on the board or display them visually, it is often in adult language. For the average and below average learner, this may create a threatening condition; after all, if a student does not understand the intended learning, mastery is unlikely to occur. Lack of mastery leads to poor self-efficacy and does not support a brain-enriched learning environment. When students clearly understand the intended learning, they know "where they are going."

Teachers learn to convert expectations into student-friendly language by defining key words in terms students understand. They learn to ask students what they think constitutes quality in a product or performance expectation, and then show how their thoughts match with the scoring guide or rubric the teacher will use to define quality. In addition, teachers can provide students with scoring guides that are written so they can understand them and can develop scoring criteria with them.

Teachers can also be taught to use models of strong and weak work—anonymous student work, work from life beyond school, and their own work. They can begin with work that demonstrates strengths and weaknesses related to problems students commonly experience, especially the problems that most concern them personally. Teachers can ask students to analyze these samples for quality and then to justify their judgments. Once teachers engage students in analyzing examples or models, they help students see a vision of what the product or performance looks like when it is done well. This again allows students to see where they are going.

Teachers must also be taught how to help students answer the question, Where am I now? and utilize two additional strategies: (1) offer regular descriptive feedback, and (2) teach students to self-assess and set goals. This is a huge paradigm shift for teachers and requires that they learn to offer descriptive feedback instead of grades on work that is for practice. Descriptive feedback should reflect student strengths and weaknesses with respect to the specific learning targets they are trying to reach. Feedback is most effective when it identifies what students are doing right, as well as what they need to work on next. All learners, especially struggling ones, need to know that they did something right, and teachers are taught to find this and label it for them, before launching into what they need to improve. Providing students with descriptive feedback is a crucial part of increasing achievement and building self-efficacy.

Teaching students to self-assess and set goals for learning is the second half of helping students answer the question, Where am I now? The leader helps teachers see that self-assessment is a necessary part of learning, not an add-on that is done if time permits or with the right students. Struggling students are the right students, as much as any others. Self-assessment includes having students do the following:

- Identify personal strengths and areas for improvement. Teachers are taught to ask students to do this before they show their work to the teacher for feedback.
- Write in a response log at the end of class, recording key points learned and questions they may have.
- Offer descriptive feedback to classmates.

Finally, teachers learn to help students answer the question, How can I close the gap? by using three additional strategies: (1) design lessons to focus on one aspect of quality at a time, (2) teach students focused revision, and (3) engage students in self-reflection and let them keep track of and share their learning. Teachers learn, when working on an expectation that has more than one aspect of quality, to build competence one block at a time. For example, mathematics problem solving requires choosing the right strategy as one component. A science experiment lab report requires a statement of the hypothesis as one component. Writing requires an introduction as one component.

In addition, teachers learn to look at the components of quality and then teach them one part at a time, making sure that students understand that all of the parts ultimately must come together. They are also taught to offer feedback focused on the component just taught, which narrows the volume of feedback students need to act on at a given time and raises their chances of success in doing so, again especially for struggling learners. This becomes a time saver for the teacher and is more instructionally powerful for students.

Furthermore, teachers are taught to show students how they would revise an answer, product, or performance and then let students revise a similar example. Teachers ask students to brainstorm advice for the (anonymous) author on how to improve the work. Then, the teacher asks students, in pairs, to revise the work using their own advice. These exercises will prepare students to work on a current product or performance of their own, revising for the aspect of quality being studied. Teachers can then give feedback on just that aspect.

Finally, teachers learn to engage students in tracking, reflecting on, and communicating about their own progress. Any activity that requires students to reflect on what they are learning and to share their progress both reinforces the learning and helps them develop insights into themselves as learners. These kinds of activities give students the opportunity to notice their own strengths, to see how far they have come, and to feel in control of the conditions of their success. By reflecting on their learning, they deepen their understanding and will remember it longer. In addition, it is the learner, not the teacher, who is doing the work.

The strategies reflect a progression that unfolds in the classroom over time. Students have trouble engaging in later steps, such as self-assessment, if they have not had experience with earlier steps, such as understanding expectations and reliably assessing work. Similarly, it is much harder for students to communicate their progress if the expectations are not clear, if they are not adept at assessing their work, and if they do not know what they need to do to improve. Taken as a systemic approach to learning in the classroom, classroom formative assessment builds self-efficacy and allows students to discover who they are as learners. Once empowered with the answer to all three questions, students achieve more, build self-efficacy, and feel the trust and safety needed in a classroom to optimize learning (Stiggins, 2006). Classroom formative assessment is brain-enriched learning.

Just as the classroom management initiative takes planning and time to implement, the same holds true for engaging the PLC in learning and implementing the classroom formative assessment strategies. However, when combined, the two initiatives create the context for a safe and trusting learning environment and one in which learning is the focus and where learning builds self-efficacy and powerful mastery experiences for students.

CONCLUSION

Leaders of PLCs need to play specific roles in order to create a learning organization that is underpinned by the twelve principles of brain/mind learning. They need to hold up the mirror to the PLC and provide them with synthesized data so members can learn how to self-analyze and self-regulate. Furthermore, they need to build human potential by creating critical collaborative structures and distributing leadership among the faculty of the PLC to help the PLC function. The outcomes of these roles build trust between the leader and the members of the PLC, and working in collaboration with each other builds staff relational trust. These conditions, in turn, lead to a collective focus and responsibility for student learning and achievement. A PLC whose members feel a sense of trust, collaboration, and cultural knowledge of their school are functioning in a brain-enriched learning organization. Once organized in this way, the attention can be turned to creating the conditions that best foster learning for students.

Two initiatives best create these conditions. Members of the PLC are carefully trained in a person-centered, humanistic classroom management paradigm and on classroom formative assessment. As shown above, these two focal points are framed in the principles of brain/mind learning and create a sense of trust, engagement, safety, and self-efficacy for students. Both initiatives must become part of the culture of the school and should not be viewed as a shot in the arm or a magic bullet. Each takes copious time, effort, and monitoring by the leader of the PLC and the members of the PLC. The dividends are rich, as both initiatives are directly tied to increasing student achievement and learning and in creating a highly functioning PLC steeped in brain-enriched learning conditions.

It is easier to "do school" from an institutionalized and behaviorist perspective, but it is certainly not effective for optimizing learning and creating the majority of students who can use their minds well. If this were so, the United States would not have a 75 percent graduation rate, and 40 percent of students entering universities and colleges would not be enrolled in remedial courses. Creating a brain-enriched learning organization is not just good for student and adult learning; it is also a moral imperative.

REFERENCES

Bandura, A. (1994). Self-efficacy. In V. S. Ramachudran (Ed.), *Encyclopedia of human behavior* (Vol. 4), (pp. 71–81). New York: Academic Press.

Caine, G., & Caine, R. N. (2010). *Strengthening and enriching your professional learning community: The art of learning together*. Reston, VA: Association for Supervision and Curriculum Development.

Caine, R. N., & Caine, G. (2011). *Natural for a connected world: Education, technology and the human brain*. New York: Teachers College Press.

Chappuis, J. (2009). *Seven strategies of assessment for learning*. Princeton, NJ: Educational Testing Service.

Conley, D. T. (2007). *Toward a more comprehensive conception of college readiness*. Eugene, OR: Educational Policy Improvement Center.

EPE Research Center. (2011). Diplomas count 2011: Beyond high school, before baccalaureate; Meaningful alternatives to a four-year degree. *Education Week, 30*(34), 1–30.

Green, J. M. (1998). Constructing the way forward for all students. A speech delivered at Innovations for Effective Schools OECD/New Zealand joint follow-up conference, Christchurch, New Zealand.

Hord, S., & Sommers, W. (2008). *Leading professional learning communities: Voices from research and practice*. Thousand Oaks, CA: Corwin.

Huffman, J. B., & Hipp, K. K. (2003). *Reculturing schools as professional learning communities*. Lanham, MD: Rowman & Littlefield.

Jones, T. B. (2013). Complexity theory. In G. Brown, B. Irby, & R. Lara-Alecio (Eds.), *Handbook of educational theories*. Charlotte, NC: Information Age Publishing.

Kohn, L. Y. (2001). A critical ethnography of the professional community in a restructured school. In P. Carspecken and G. Walford (Eds.), *Critical ethnography and education* (pp. 119–152). Amsterdam: JAI Press.

Marzano, R. J. (2003). *Classroom management that works: Research-based strategies for every teacher.* Alexandria, VA: Association for Supervision and Curriculum Development.

Newmann, F. M. (1996). *Authentic achievement: Restructuring schools for intellectual quality.* San Francisco: Jossey-Bass.

Newmann, F. M., & Oliver, D. W. (1967). Education and community. *Harvard Educational Review, 37*(1), 61–106.

Popham, W. J. (2008). *Transformative assessment.* Alexandria, VA: Association for Supervision and Curriculum Development.

Stiggins, R. (2006). *Introduction to student involved assessment to learning.* Upper Saddle River, NJ: Prentice Hall.

Wang, M. C., Haertel, G. D., & Walberg H. J. (1993). Toward a knowledge base for school learning. *Review of Educational Research, 63*, 249–294.

Chapter Eight

Schematic for Implementation

Creating the "Cogito" for Innovative Schools

Ross B. Sherman

ALICE: Would you tell me please which way I ought to go from here?
CHESHIRE: That depends a great deal on where you want to get to.
ALICE: I don't much care where—
CHESHIRE: Then it doesn't matter which way you go.
ALICE: . . . so long as I get somewhere.
CHESHIRE: Oh, you're sure to do that—if you only walk long enough.

—Lewis Carroll (2000)

An old adage says, "Plan to succeed or fail to plan." Almost every educator has attended workshops and seminars that were informative, motivational, and inspirational, but they have not been transformational. The question is why? In most instances the workshop or seminar did not provide a vehicle to transform intention into reality. Developing, implementing, and facilitating a fundamental change in beliefs of an organization, particularly an educational enterprise that is steeped in tradition, takes careful planning, commitment, and a fluid plan of execution. It is not for the faint of heart. The meek will not inherit the school!

In Latin, the term "cogito" means to think, ruminate, ponder, consider, and plan. This chapter will provide a schema and tools for planning and implementing natural, brain-compatible learning in schools. It can also include any other initiatives for school change and improvement. The key to improving schools lies in the development and implementation of a carefully thought-out, ongoing plan, or "Cogito for Innovative Schools," that actively involves the Professional Learning Community (PLC) discussed in the previous chapter.

Planning is an attempt to articulate the direction an organization should pursue and is one of the most important functions for the success of the enterprise. Planning should be pervasive and impact all areas of an organization. For instance, school districts typically have long-range plans in the areas of facilities, finance, and personnel to ensure those functions will be successful in meeting the demands of the organization in those areas.

A school or school district should have a long-range plan for school improvement. The plan should be projected in three- to five-year intervals and answer the question, Where do we want our organization to be in five years? The development of the plan requires conversations, collaborations, consensus, and commitment among faculty and staff. Those four C's are processes that facilitate the development of a Cogito for Innovative Schools that is thoughtful, inclusive, long range, and likely to be implemented.

The educational leader should assume responsibility for facilitating the plan in his or her particular leadership capacity. However, the plan should be developed collaboratively with the faculty and other stakeholders. This assumes that the faculty is a community of scholars and has a professional responsibility to engage in activities that promote the success of the enterprise. To facilitate the development of the Cogito for Innovative Schools, a core planning committee should be identified consisting of key personnel who represent the various academic units within the school. The core planning committee would develop the components of the plan and present it to the entire faculty for review and adoption.

In essence, the Cogito for Innovative Schools provides the road map for the implementation of school-improvement plans. For instance, if your objective was to drive to a distant city, you would not begin the excursion without a GPS system or a map. The Cogito for Innovative Schools can be the map that guides the implementation of the school restructuring. In addition, it provides a method of monitoring the implementation and ultimately measuring the success of the school restructuring.

COGITO FOR INNOVATIVE SCHOOLS MODEL

Emmanuel Lasker, the second world chess champion from Germany, wrote that "a bad plan is better than no plan." Lasker knew that in life, as in chess, there are many forces at work, many contingencies and variables.

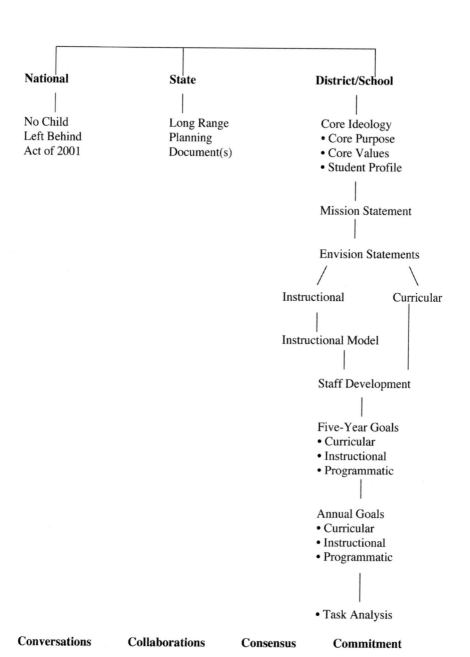

National

No Child
Left Behind
Act of 2001

State

Long Range
Planning
Document(s)

District/School

Core Ideology
• Core Purpose
• Core Values
• Student Profile

Mission Statement

Envision Statements

Instructional   Curricular

Instructional Model

Staff Development

Five-Year Goals
• Curricular
• Instructional
• Programmatic

Annual Goals
• Curricular
• Instructional
• Programmatic

• Task Analysis

Conversations   **Collaborations**   **Consensus**   **Commitment**

Figure 8.1. *Cogito* **for innovative schools' model.**

Having a plan helped one focus one's attention and skill in an intentional way. In this manner, one could be proactive as opposed to reactive. Similarly, planning for schools does not exist in a vacuum. An effective plan takes into account all contributing factors and influences. Indeed, in order to effectively plan and implement the logistics, one must know the hierarchical strata of the overall system and subsystems. The school is part of a larger system that comprises the district, the district is part of the state system, and finally the states constitute the national system of education. Therefore, we need to understand the environmental context in which we operate before we can engage in planning for a district or campus. Figure 8.1 presents the Cogito for Innovative Schools model showing how the national, state, and local components interface.

NATIONAL STANDARDS AND GOALS

An appropriate jumping-off point for planning is to ask what is the national agenda for education. Historically, education has been a state function locally administered. While early founders of our democracy such as Thomas Jefferson and Horace Mann advocated strongly for public education, there is nothing in the U.S. Constitution that creates such an institution. Rather, public education falls under the Tenth Amendment: "The powers not delegated to the United States by the Constitution, nor prohibited by it to the States, are reserved to the States respectively, or to the people."

The federal government involvement has been limited to programs that received federal funding, such as special education, career and technology, and compensatory education. In essence, there have been fifty different educational systems operating fairly independently. However, with the advent of Goals 2000 in the early 1990s, a national agenda for education was outlined. Subsequently, this has been replaced with the No Child Left Behind Act of 2001 (NCLB). The NCLB legislation has four major thrusts:

1. Stronger accountability for results
2. More flexibility for states and communities

3. Use of proven educational methods
4. More choices for parents

The national agenda for education provides the context in which schools operate. Therefore, it is important to understand the national expectations before engaging in the development of a plan for a campus or district.

STATE STANDARDS AND GOALS

The next element of the environmental scan would be a review of any state long-range planning documents. As previously stated, education is a state function falling under the Tenth Amendment. It is not by accident that all fifty states have a provision for public education within their state constitution. The importance of education to our society is readily apparent. Indeed, every election year the topic of education is at the forefront.

Therefore, it is essential to consider that each individual state may or may not have an educational long-range plan. Each state is different on policy and educational focus at any one time, but most include at least a standardized state curriculum. Likewise, most states include an accountability system centered on high-stakes, standardized testing. Therefore, the next step is to secure and review any state documents that articulate the educational plan and long-term goals for the state.

DISTRICT OR SCHOOL STANDARDS AND POLICY

Once the review of the federal and state documents is complete, the emphasis shifts to the individual district or school. The first component in the Cogito for Innovative Schools is the articulation of a core ideology. The core ideology answers the question, What do we believe as a school in this district? It consists of a core purpose statement, a set of core values, and a comprehensive student profile.

Core Purpose

The core purpose is a concise statement that addresses the question of why the organization exists today and why it will exist in the future. Examples of core purposes (Collins & Parras, 2004) for different organizations include the following:

- 3M—To solve problems innovatively
- Mary Kay Cosmetics—To give unlimited opportunities to women
- Walt Disney—To make people happy
- Wal-Mart—To give ordinary folks the chance to buy the same things as rich people
- Nike—To experience the emotion of competition, winning, and crushing competitors

The first task of the core planning committee is to articulate why the school or district exists and what benefit it provides to the local community. Answering these two questions creates a definition for the organization and can help concretize the school's or district's purpose into measurable goals.

Core Values

The second component of the core ideology is a set of core values. The core values are a set of guiding principles that define what an organization stands for and how people should behave in pursuit of the core purpose. The core value statements should focus on areas critical for success of the enterprise. Core values help shape decision making such as the critical task of whom to hire to contribute to the success of the organization. They provide a litmus test for making difficult choices between competing ideas or factions. For instance, a school could develop core value statements in the following areas:

- School or organization
- Teaching and learning
- Children or students
- Curriculum, instruction, and assessment

The next task for the core committee is to determine the values the school holds in common that will guide the actions of the faculty and staff. For illustration purposes, the examples focus on what an educational

School/Organization

- We will promote a safe and positive atmosphere for all students.
- We will provide equitable educational opportunities for all students.
- We will provide opportunities for parent and community involvement.

Teaching/Learning

- We will create exemplary standards of teaching and learning.
- We will incorporate brain-compatible learning in our teaching.
- We will encourage and provide opportunities for professional growth in the area of brain-compatible learning for faculty and staff.
- We will meet the individual needs of all students.

Children/Students

- We will model the character values of pride, cooperation, responsibility, respect, integrity, and citizenship.
- We will create life long learners.
- We will foster attributes that will enable students to be productive, educated citizens within the community.

Curriculum/Instruction/Assessment

- We will use Best Practices in curriculum.
- We will use brain-enriched instructional practices.
- We will use multiple formats for assessment.
- We will align the curriculum, instruction, and assessment.

Adopted by *Anywhere Innovative Elementary School*: (Date)

Conversations   **Collaborations**   **Consensus**   **Commitment**

Figure 8.2. *Anywhere innovative elementary* **core values.**

leader might use in leading a campus to become a learning organization that utilizes brain-enriched principles. Figure 8.2 presents an example of core values for a school.

Comprehensive Student Profile

The third component in the core ideology is to develop a comprehensive student profile. This profile identifies the skills, abilities, and outcomes a student will possess as a result of his or her experiences at the school. Thus, the profile forms a compact with the community and parents and makes a promise. As a result of your child's experiences at our school, your child will possess the following skills, abilities, and outcomes:

• Intellectual abilities
• Academic skills
• Social skills
• Emotional skills
• Physical skills

The third task in which the core committee will engage is the identification of the specific skills, abilities, and attributes students will possess when they leave the school. What will a successful student look like? How will we know if we have been successful? What will our students be able to do or achieve? Figure 8.3 presents an example of a comprehensive student profile.

The development of a core ideology is a critical component of the Cogito for Innovative Schools. It requires thoughtful dialogue of all stakeholders to come to consensus with regard to fundamental beliefs and values that will guide the organization in all decisions that impact the school and its students. Take whatever time is necessary to build a consensus of these beliefs and values. The time invested at the development stage will produce dividends during implementation.

COGITO FOR INNOVATIVE SCHOOLS: CAMPUS LEVEL

Planning at the school level is where the rubber hits the road. The development of a successful campus-level plan requires critical conversations, collaborations, consensus, and commitment. The core planning committee creates the components of the plan, which is subsequently submitted to the entire faculty and staff for discussion and adoption. It is here where ideology becomes reality, where theory morphs into practice. The campus planning committee will be charged with solving the minute logistical challenges that can make or break a successful implementation of the plan. Here is where attention to detail and a system of feedback among the staff and the committee will be of the utmost importance.

Children/students will possess the following skills/abilities/outcomes as a result of their experiences at Anywhere Innovative Early Learning Academy:

Intellectual Abilities

- To solve both academic and social problems.
- To recognize the relationships between self and community.
- To think independently.

Academic Skills

- To solve problems using available resources.
- To be prepared academically to succeed at the next level.

Emotional Skills

- To express feeling/concerns in an appropriate manner.
- To accept challenges and be competent in their abilities to solve them.

Social Skills

- To act appropriately based upon social situations.
- To use words rather than actions to solve problems.
- To consider the feelings of others.
- To work cooperatively in a group.

Physical Skills

- To display appropriate fine/gross motor skills.
- To promote lifelong fitness and good health.

Adopted by *Anywhere Innovative Early Learning Academy*: (Date)

Conversations   Collaborations   Consensus   Commitment

Figure 8.3.   *Anywhere innovative early learning academy* **comprehensive student profile.**

Mission Statement

The mission statement is the bedrock of the organization and answers the question, What are we called to do? It is a statement that tells what the organization is and what the organization does. Avoid terms or phrases that tend to simply be buzzwords or clichés, as they will only dilute the real mission desired. There are many mission statements in schools today that claim a learner-centered environment as the mission, yet walking down the hall makes it painfully obvious that learning and student activity is teacher centered. An example of a mission statement would be the following:

> The "Anywhere Innovative School" community will help each child develop his or her potential intellectually, academically, socially, emotionally, and physically in a natural and lifelong way.

During the development of the mission statement, the core planning committee should seek input from all stakeholders including teachers, parents, community members, and business members. All too often, mission statements are developed, hung on the wall, and quickly forgotten. The mission statement should be revisited on a regular basis and updated periodically.

Instructional Envision Statements

Instructional envision statements are the guiding principles for how we teach. The principles should reflect brain-enriched strategies and transcend grade levels and academic disciplines. This part of plan development will require the most reflection by stakeholders on what instructional practices are best for students as opposed to which ones are most easily delivered by teachers. Research makes it clear that many of the instructional methods that were used by most teachers are not the latest and best technologies and methods for learners today. The developmental process of the school's Cogito for Innovative Schools must confront this reality and immerse the learning community in current best practices and brain-compatible learning literature.

Typically, the instructional envision statements will consist of approximately ten statements that begin with "We believe." The statements reflect the fundamental beliefs and serve as a guide for implementing brain-enriched instruction in the classroom. The core committee will identify the brain-compatible, research-supported instructional principles that will be implemented in each classroom. Figure 8.4 presents an example of a set of instructional envision statements.

Curricular Envision Statements

Curricular envision statements are guiding principles for what we teach. These principles are discipline specific and require a set for each aca-

We believe:

- in utilizing brain-compatible research techniques.
- in providing instruction at the correct level of difficulty.
- in making learning real, relevant, and meaningful to students.
- in integrating higher-level thinking skills throughout all disciplines.
- in engaging students in complex content by teaching concepts, principles, generalizations, and theories.
- in using inquiry-based and collaborative learning models.
- in utilizing project-based interdisciplinary, instructional approaches.
- in incorporating technology across the curriculum.
- in creating a motivational environment in the classroom by using the factors of success, interest, feeling tone, level of concern, knowledge of results, and rewards.
- in providing practice sessions that are short, intense, and highly motivating

Adopted by *Anywhere Innovative High School*: (Date)

Conversations   Collaborations   Consensus   Commitment

Figure 8.4. *Anywhere innovative high school* **instructional envision statements.**

demic discipline in the school's curriculum. The core planning committee should delegate the development of envision statements for each discipline to subcommittees consisting of teachers from each grade level at the elementary level or the department at the secondary level. For instance, there would be a subcommittee for mathematics, natural sciences, social sciences, fine arts, and so forth.

Each subcommittee would be charged with developing approximately ten statements that begin with "We believe." These statements would be discipline specific, transcend all courses in the discipline, and articulate the fundamental beliefs about that curricular area.

The core planning committee can assist with the development of curricular envision statements by providing the subcommittees with any national reports and state documents for the area. For instance, the International Reading Association publishes the *Standards for Reading Professionals* (2010), and the National Council for the Social Studies produces *National Curriculum Standards for Social Studies: A Framework for Teaching, Learning, and Assessment* (2010). These reports address the recommendations of experts in the respective fields, and similar reports exist for most academic disciplines. In addition to reviewing the recommendations of professional organizations, the "Common Core State

• We believe in a curriculum that is manipulative based using multi-sensory techniques.
• We believe that mathematical learning should move from concrete to abstract levels of understanding.
• We believe in creating representations to make abstract ideas more concrete and build understanding of concepts.
• We believe in discussing, reading, and writing about mathematics.
• We believe in using word problems with multiple structures and solution paths.
• We believe in using open-ended problems and extended problem-solving projects.
• We believe in justifying answers and solution processes in mathematics.
• We believe in connecting mathematics to other subjects and the real world.
• We believe inductive and deductive reasoning should be incorporated into mathematical teaching.
• We believe that technology should be applied to the mathematics curriculum.

Adopted by *Anywhere Innovative Elementary School*: (Date)

Conversations   Collaborations   Consensus   Commitment

Figure 8.5.   *Anywhere innovative elementary school* mathematics envision statements.

Standards" (Council of Chief State School Officers, 2012), in English-language arts and mathematics, has been adopted by most states and articulates what students should learn as a result of their K–12 experience.

Each subcommittee is asked to present their recommendations to the entire faculty for review and adoption. Figure 8.5 presents an example of a set of mathematics curricular envision statements.

Instructional Model

The next phase in the planning process is the development of an instructional model. The instructional model is based on brain-enriched teaching principles that have been substantiated through research and practice as promoting student achievement. In chapter 4, the argument was made that a constructivist instructional model is the easiest way to support brain-compatible learning. The instructional principles developed should be generic and transcend all academic disciplines and grade levels.

The topics within the instructional model form a foundational knowledge that all teachers should possess. It provides the teacher with a repertoire of brain-compatible skills to draw upon during a constructivist instructional process and philosophy. In addition, the instructional model serves as the

- Brain-Compatible Learning Principles
- Constructivism
- Erickson's Structure of Knowledge
- Bloom's Taxonomy
- Motivation Theory
- Questioning Strategies
- Cooperative Learning
- Inquiry-Based Practices
- Multiple Intelligences
- Time on Task
- Retention Theory
- Practice Theory

Adopted by *Anywhere Innovative School*: (Date)

Conversations   **Collaborations**   **Consensus**   **Commitment**

Figure 8.6. *Anywhere innovative school* instructional paradigm.

basis for designing the instructional strand of the staff development program. Figure 8.6 presents an example of an instructional model.

Staff Development Principles

The staff development model is designed to provide teachers with the instructional pedagogy, curricular knowledge, and classroom management skills necessary to facilitate academic achievement in the classroom. The critical attributes to effective staff development are that it should be as follows:

- Correlated with success in the classroom: Addresses areas that promote student achievement
- Systematic: Ensures that all teachers receive the common core of instructional, curricular, and discipline management training
- Long range: Planned in 3–5-year increments

The first element in creating a staff development model is that it should be correlated with success in the classroom. In essence, if you were going to design or develop a master teacher, what expertise would he or she possess? One could suggest that a master teacher possess the following skills and abilities:

1. Instructional expertise: Using brain-enriched instructional principles that maximize student learning
2. Curricular knowledge: Incorporating research-based, brain-enriched best practices in specific disciplines of study
3. Classroom management skills: Organizing the classroom into a productive learning environment
4. Human relations skills: Interacting effectively with students
5. Work ethic: Committing to work diligently to improve instructional and curricular effectiveness

The next element in creating a comprehensive staff development model is that it should be systematic from year to year. A common lament from principals to new teachers is, "You should have been here last year. We had this great staff development session." If the staff development was deemed to be beneficial for last year's faculty, shouldn't new teachers also receive the same staff development?

The final component is that staff development should be long range. Unfortunately, some principals plan staff development from session to session. However, a comprehensive staff development program would be projected in 3–5-year increments and be recurring so as to address new hires and remediation from year to year.

Staff Development Model

Figure 8.7 presents a schematic for creating a staff development model that is systematic, long range, and correlated to success in the classroom. The vertical axis reflects the days that are set aside for staff development activities. Each day is divided into a morning and afternoon session. The horizontal axis (phases) equates to the years the teacher is employed by the school. For instance, phase 1 would be the first year of employment by the school. Each year the teacher would move to the next phase and year.

The next step in completing the staff development model is to annually identify days for curricular and classroom management staff development. The specific topics for these days are derived from the curricular envision

	Phase I	Phase II	Phase III	Phase IV
Day 1 – a.m.	Welcome Back / State-Mandated Activities			
Day 1 – p.m.	Brain-Compatible Research	Motivation Theory	Learning Styles	Individual
Day 2 – a.m.	Discipline Management Topics			
Day 2 – p.m.	Inquiry Model	Bloom's Taxonomy	Retention Theory	Individual
Day 3 – a.m.	Curricular Topics			
Day 3 – a.m.	Cooperative Learning	Erickson's Structure of Knowledge	Practice Theory	Individual
Day 4 – a.m.	Curricular Topics			
Day 4 – p.m.	Multiple Intelligences	Transfer Theory	Diagnosis & Evaluation	Individual

SYSTEMATIC, LONG-RANGE PLAN CORRELATED WITH SUCCESS IN THE CLASSROOM

Adopted by *Anywhere Innovative School*: (Date)

Conversations   Collaborations   Consensus   Commitment

Figure 8.7. *Anywhere innovative school* staff development model.

statements and curricular goals identified in the Cogito for Innovative Schools document. For instance, teachers in specific disciplines could meet within the district or school to have content-related staff development.

Once the curriculum and discipline management days are identified, the next step is to plot the topics from the instructional model into the staff development plan. The model can be fully implemented by using in-house personnel to present the various sessions. Different topics are assigned to teachers and administrators who will become the primary presenters of that topic. The advantage of this approach is that it creates teacher leaders among the presenters.

Five-Year Goals

A set of five-year goals should be developed in the areas of instruction, curriculum, and programs. Goals provide a vehicle for focusing the aforementioned areas. The instructional goal would be to implement the instructional model previously discussed and outlined in the staff development model.

In curriculum, a broad goal statement should be developed for each discipline of study. Examples of goal statements are as follows:

• We will create an exemplary math program by implementing a manipulative-based approach that moves from the concrete to the abstract and builds upon prior knowledge. (Elementary Mathematics)
• We will create an exemplary science program through cross-curricular teaching of science concepts and scientific methods as well as technology to enhance the discovery and inquiry method of scientific investigation. (Secondary Science)

Once each of the curricular goal statements is identified, then each goal is task analyzed by asking the following questions:

1. What instructional resources are required (capital outlay and materials)?
2. What staff development is required?
3. What personnel are required?
4. What facilities are required?

This helps the principal in allocating resources to achieve the goals identified. Figures 8.8 and 8.9 present a set of five-year goals and an example of a task analysis of one of the goals.

The final area of goal setting addresses programmatic goals. These are areas not addressed in the instructional or curricular goals and may include programs, facilities, or personnel. An example of programmatic goals might include the following:

1. Developing a service-learning program at a high school
2. Adding a counselor to the school
3. Establishing a parent center at a school

Figure 8.10 presents an example set of programmatic goals for an innovative school.

Instruction

- To implement the school's instructional t model.
- To train all professional staff in the use of brain-compatible teaching methods.

Curriculum

- To develop a literature-based reading program.
- To develop a manipulative-based mathematics program.
- To develop a spelling program based on high-frequency and content words.
- To develop an appreciation for the Spanish language.
- To develop an experimental and discovery approach to science.
- To develop musical concepts through a multisensory approach to music.
- To integrate technology into the classroom.
- To develop physical skills based on personal growth and development.
- To instruct all students in problem-solving, higher-level thinking, and research skills.

Program

- To create a series of enrichment clubs to meet the diverse needs of the multitalented learner.
- To expand our summer enrichment program.
- To develop parent education programs.
- To continue and expand our community service projects.

Adopted by *Anywhere Innovative Elementary School*: (Date)

Conversations   Collaborations   Consensus   Commitment

Figure 8.8.   *Anywhere innovative elementary* school five-year goals.

CONCLUSION

It is an incredible time to be an educational leader! As a principal or other instructional administrator, your primary responsibility is to plan the educational program for your school or division. With the advent of brain-enriched research, you have an opportunity and the moral obligation to develop each of your teachers, so they meet the intellectual, academic, and social-emotional needs of all students. The development and ongoing use of the Cogito for Innovative Schools provides you with a systematic model for accomplishing this goal and a living written plan to help you communicate to all internal and external stakeholders where the campus or program is heading. Each step is critical for long-term systemic change, and the school leader must commit to the time necessary to build widespread consensus among the PLC. It is a big task to fundamentally change

We will create an exemplary math program by developing a brain-enriched and manipulative-based mathematics program.

Instructional Resources
- Math Enrichment Lab
  - Twenty computer stations
  - Twenty iPads
  - One presentation center
  - One Smart Board
  - Class set of manipulatives for each grade level
  - Math games
  - Computer software
  - Class set of calculators
  - Class set of dry erase boards and markers
- Individual Classrooms
  - Demonstration teaching center
  - 20 class sets of base ten blocks
  - 20 class sets of pattern blocks
  - 20 class sets of tangrams
  - 20 class sets of fraction sets
  - 20 class sets of geoboards
  - 20 class sets of Cuisenaire rods
  - 20 class sets of geometric solids
  - 20 class sets of calculators
  - Computer software for classroom computers

Staff Development
- Train staff in math manipulatives
- Train staff in software
- Train staff in problem-solving strategies
- Send lead teacher to NCTM Annual Conference

Personnel
- Teacher for Math Enrichment Lab

Facilities
- Locate and establish a classroom for the Math Enrichment Lab

Adopted by *Anywhere Innovative Elementary School*: (Date)

Conversations   **Collaborations**   **Consensus**   **Commitment**

Figure 8.9.   *Anywhere innovative elementary school* **five-year goal task analysis.**

what a campus or academic department and its teachers do day-to-day to facilitate learning. Time invested up front in immersion of the PLC with current literature on brain-compatible learning will help the dialogue and provide the reflection necessary to build a strong instructional consensus. Good leaders know that failing to plan is planning to fail. It takes deliberate actions and commitment by strong and focused leadership.

• To create a series of enrichment clubs to meet the diverse needs of the multitalented learner.
• To expand our summer enrichment program.
• To develop parent education programs.
• To continue and expand our community service projects.

Adopted by *Anywhere Innovative Elementary School*: (Date)

Conversations   **Collaborations**   **Consensus**   **Commitment**

Figure 8.10. *Anywhere innovative elementary school* **five-year goals programmatic.**

REFERENCES

Carroll, L. (2000). *Alice's adventures in wonderland and through the looking glass*. New York: Penguin Putnam.

Collins, J., & Parras, J. (2004). *Built to last: Successful habits of visionary companies*. New York: Harper Business Publishers.

Council of Chief State School Officers. (2012). Common core state standards. Retrieved August 27, 2012, from http://www.corestandards.org/about-the-standards.

International Reading Association and National Council of Teachers of English. (2010). *Standards for reading professionals*. Urbana, IL: Author.

National Council for the Social Studies. (2010). *National curriculum standards for social studies: A framework for teaching, learning, and assessment*. Silver Springs, MD: Author.

Texas Administrative Code (TAC). (2012). Title 19, Part II, Chapters 110–128, Texas Essential Knowledge and Skills. Retrieved December 3 from http://info. sos.state.tx.us/pls/pub/readtac$ext.ViewTAC?tac_view=3&ti=19&pt=2.

Texas Education Agency. (2011). Texas Education Agency Strategic Plan: For fiscal years 2011–2015. Austin: Author. Retrieved December 1, 2013, from http://www.tea.state.tx.us/index2.aspx?id=2147485142.

U.S. Department of Education. (2001). No Child Left Behind Act (NCLB). Washington, DC: Author. Retrieved August 29, 2012, from http://www2 .ed.gov/nclb/overview/importance/edpicks.jhtml?src=ln.

Chapter Nine

The Courage to Lead

The Knowledge to Succeed

Peggy B. Gill

Come to the edge.
We might fall.
Come to the edge.
It's too high!
COME TO THE EDGE!
And they came
And he pushed
And they flew!

—Christopher Logue (1969)

Leadership is a complex process that fascinates people. Any discussion of schools will include references to the leadership of each school. People bemoan the resignation of a "good principal," question the leadership abilities of an incoming principal, and endlessly discuss what is good or bad about leadership styles. A clearer example of this fascination can be found by looking at the head coach of any football team. After a brief survey of the talent on the team, the discussion quickly turns to the leadership skills of the head coach. There is an assumed connection between the success of the team and the leadership ability of the coach. Can the coach bring the team together? Can the coach encourage talent? Does the coach inspire greatness in the players? All of these questions, couched slightly differently, are also asked about school leaders. But what is leadership?

Leadership is a continuously evolving concept, and there are a wide variety of definitions of good leadership. The twentieth century saw the evolution of leadership theories through trait theory, behaviorist theory, situational leadership theory, transformational leadership theory, and systemic strategic leadership theory (Green, 2013). More recently theorists have added servant leadership (Greenleaf, 2002) and spirituality (Kouzes & Posner, 2007). Throughout all these definitions is the common theme of leadership as a process of influencing others to achieve a goal. This goal, or vision, is achieved through the cooperative and collaborative activities of others. Thus, leadership is relational.

The relational activities of leaders occur in a specific context. This context provides the information leaders need to adjust behaviors to encourage others to achieve their goal. Matt Ridley (1996) suggests that people are hardwired to work together to achieve the common good. The leader's challenge is to inspire followers to make real changes that will achieve both tangible goals and a higher purpose.

As further understanding of the context of leadership, consider Gregory Bateson's (1970) discussion of the separation between how people think and the reality of the natural world. In his lecture at the Nineteenth Annual Korzybski Memorial Lecture, Bateson began by referring to Korzybski's distinction between map and territory. Bateson took this opportunity to expand on his view that people generally fail to distinguish between the symbols used to represent reality and reality as it may exist. This failure leads almost inevitably to errors of logical typing, erroneous perceptions of cause-effect relations, and deficient understandings of the impact of the observer (i.e., leader) on the system as a whole (Russell, 1956; Whitehead & Russell, 1910).

In a similar vein, Fritjof Capra (1982) highlights the critical role of what he terms "a new notion of causality" (p. 85). Although classical science and Western thought in general is constructed by the Cartesian method of analyzing the world into component parts for analysis and understanding of the "causal laws" of nature, Capra explains that the notion of separate parts to any structure, living or otherwise, at best has only approximate validity—those parts are not connected by causal laws in the traditional sense. The structure of matter is not mechanical, and the structure of mind is at least similar to that of matter. To borrow Capra's term, the universe is an "interconnected web of relationships," and leadership, if it is to be effective, must draw heavily upon this understanding and its implications.

Today we recognize that leadership is a natural process that occurs throughout the biological world, a process in which individual elements influence other elements to achieve a common goal of survival. It is how nature works. Nature is comprised of or organized into systems (Dickman & Blair, 2002). People likewise operate in systems and must use the intelligence of the system to lead successful change.

CHANGE PROCESS

All leaders recognize that change is inevitable. After all, school leaders have usually spent several years in the classroom. They are familiar with the change in accountability requirements, the change in curriculum, and the change in district leadership. Change is a familiar quantity to school leaders. However, how the leader views change is important. Here are several models of change that can help the leader use the potential of change to achieve results. Kurt Lewin (1947) suggests that change is a three-step process:

1. Unfreezing: The process of convincing the group that change is needed and that the attitudes and beliefs that are currently in place are no longer valid or sufficient.
2. Change to the new level of belief: This involves changing the current perceptions of oneself and of the organization. This is a basic restructuring of how the brain perceives reality.
3. Freezing at a new level: This process ensures that the change is permanent and is now hardwired into the organization.

Elizabeth Kubler-Ross Model

This is a very linear approach and may not be fully consistent with how people progress through change. To address this linearity, Elizabeth Kubler-Ross (1997) proposed a five-step process of change that acknowledges everyone may progress at different rates and may skip some stages. The five stages Kubler-Ross suggests were first presented around death and dying but have good application for any great change:

1. Denial and isolation: Almost everyone uses this approach when first confronted with major change.

2. Anger: Anger may be expressed at the leader, others who support the change, or the organization as a whole.
3. Bargaining: Teachers may bargain in subtle ways, for example, "I'll try this new technique, but let me keep my textbook and lectures." It is a coping strategy to avoid seeing the full magnitude of the change.
4. Depression: Change always involves loss. Teachers are losing their familiar strategies and teaching approaches. This may result in some loss of enthusiasm for teaching.
5. Acceptance: The change is now "how we do things here."

Change as Transition

William Bridges (2009) focuses on the transition process that takes place within the individual teacher. He proposes that change is external but transition is the internal reactions to the change. His phases are not linear, and any teacher may move back and forth between the phases.

1. Ending: Teachers must let go of a piece of their identify as they move into new ways of teaching.
2. Shifting into the neutral zone: This phase is full of confusion and uncertainty and may be the most difficult phase for teachers. It is a time of chaos and therefore, while very challenging, also offers the most opportunity for creativity. Innovation will most likely occur in this phase.
3. New beginning: In this phase, teachers are moving forward and adopting new ways of teaching and new ways of thinking about learning. Teachers will only achieve this phase if they can see that risk is rewarded and not punished in the school.

Kotter's Process of Change

John Kotter (2012) provides a view of change that is widely used in business and organizational change management. This model focuses on "the doing" of change rather than the emotional responses to change. It can be very effective when coupled with the "understanding" of change.

1. Create a sense of urgency. Teachers must understand why teaching practices need to change to be brain compatible.

2. Identify your guiding team. Identify the people on your campus who share your vision and will commit to the hard work it takes to implement change.
3. Create visions and strategies. The vision must clearly serve to drive the change. Teachers want to know where the school and leadership team are going.
4. Communicate for buy-in. Keep the vision at the top of the agenda at all times. Constantly remind teachers why we are making the changes.
5. Empower people. Encourage teachers to take risks, try new strategies, and participate in designing the new approach. Put in a range of supports so your teachers can act on the vision.
6. Produce short-term wins. This is critical. Point out successes. Building in short-term wins allows teachers to feel accomplishment and to see that the changes can work.
7. Build momentum. Celebrate successes in your organization. Use these successes to energize your faculty and staff. Select the next steps in the process based on these wins so the faculty can see the continuity of the process.
8. Nurture the new culture. Continue to recognize and support the efforts of faculty to implement new ideas.

Peter Senge: A Systems Approach to Change

Peter Senge's (2006) model of change is part of his work on the learning organization presented in *The Fifth Discipline*. Senge encourages leaders to use the natural world as a base for thinking about change. Thus, the whole system is important and evolves through interactions with other systems. He views change in schools as too complex to plan in great detail. Rather, he suggests leaders work with the evolving system. Senge's principles of change include the following:

1. Start small.
2. Grow steadily.
3. Don't try to plan everything.
4. Expect challenges.

Leaders who anticipate that there will be challenges to the change are not overwhelmed by these challenges but see them as a logical progression through the change process.

LEADERSHIP AND THE BRAIN

Understanding change and the change process is only one part of developing the courage to lead. In addition, today's principal must understand how the brain works as well as the implications for leadership. The age-old question is how the mind and the brain are related. In the West, people tend to identify the brain as our thinking organ and the heart as our feeling organ. However, currently no one can say exactly how a "thought" develops.

In fact, an understanding of the brain is informed by many disciplines: neuroscience, anthropology, and developmental psychology, for example. An integration of the information from all these fields brings forth neural responses, emotions, memory, interpersonal relationships, and context as important to understanding the mind (Siegel, 2012).

The human brain is an amazing, complex organ that has evolved from simple survival to learning, and finally to higher-order thinking skills. Unlike other mammals, the human brain's cerebrum comprises over 80 percent of the brain and contains the network of cells that allow conscious and complex reasoning. In addition, the human brain retains communication with the spinal cord and the rest of the body, as well as the limbic system, which gives the capacity for learning, memory, and emotional response. The brain is a multifaceted but single organ.

Daniel Siegel (2012) states, "To put it simply, human connections shape neural connections" (p. 3). What are the implications for leadership from what we are learning about these connections in the brain?

- The human brain is complex, with incredible environmental responsiveness.
- The human brain is social.
- The human brain is emotional.
- The brain seeks patterns.
- The human brain reflects.

The Brain Is Complex and Responsive

The human brain is a complex system that responds to input from the environment. The success of the brain derives not from the individual parts of the brain but from how those parts interact. Patterns are established through this interaction that result in an individual, self-organized mind (Siegel, 2012). These patterns then result in further organization as new stimuli appear. As groups of people work together, further complexity results. Neural pathways, even in adults, may be added, modified, or even deleted in response to environmental interactions.

In addition to being a complex system, the brain is nonlinear. Thus, small changes in the environment may result in major changes in brain development. The leader's behaviors influence the environmental experiences and thus have the potential to either stimulate growth in others or lessen the chance of development. This may range from something as simple as water and food provided at meetings, to facilitating serious dialogue about the school's vision.

The Brain Is Social

The human brain has evolved through a wealth of social interactions. Remember that the main task of cells in your brain is to survive. Your genes organize into societies to ensure their genetic codes are passed on. Social interaction and cooperation are intertwined at the genetic level of all living things. As people evolved, the obvious advantage of living in social groups emerged. The human brain was refined and expanded through the development of communication, tools, and memory. Each of these developments contributed to an ever-expanding complexity. We are continuing to learn about how this social development of the brain occurs; however, the basic premise that human intelligence has been strongly influenced by social interaction is commonly accepted (Rock & Page, 2009). Thus, a courageous leader recognizes this need for social interaction and provides multiple opportunities for faculty and staff to interact, share ideas, and solve problems collectively.

The Brain Is Emotional

The human brain is able to remember not only events in the past but also the emotions associated with those events. When you think about a childhood incident that was pleasant, you feel pleasure. This is the result of emotions attached to those experiences within the brain. As mentioned above, the brain is all about survival. Emotion stands at the forefront of this struggle for survival. Emotions serve to focus attention on events, assess the merits of these events, and decide what action or inaction is necessary. Emotions allow you to judge whether an event is good or an event is bad. If you smell a carton of milk in the refrigerator and it has an horrific odor, that's bad and you do not drink the milk. If you open a present and get exactly what you wanted, that's good and it makes you happy. Emotion allows rational thought. People who are injured in the area of the brain associated with emotion are limited in their ability to think rationally.

Courageous leaders should recognize that the brain is emotional and emotions cannot be stopped. However, at the same time, emotions are what build emotional commitment to the school vision and mission. It is the leader's responsibility to create the circumstances that will arouse this emotional response to the school's vision.

The Brain Is Pattern Seeking

The brain seeks patterns as part of the survival processes (Schwartz, 2002). Organization of information into meaningful patterns allows the brain to construct knowledge. The brain constructs multiple layers of patterns. For example, when you say the word "airplane," you have an embedded pattern based on your experience that includes the sounds of different planes, the multiple words for plane such as "jet" and "helicopter," the shape and parts of an airplane, and the planes on which you have flown. All of these patterns combine to make the larger pattern for "airplane" and the meaning you ascribe to the concept. As we interact with the world, our brain naturally updates and adjusts these patterns through modifications and strengthening of neural pathways. These patterns are the way people organize their world and their understanding of how it works. While it may, at first, seem simple to understand how someone else's brain works, these patterns are actually different for every person. For the leader, these differences in patterns become very important. The leader must help everyone in the school create patterns that are similar in understanding. Also, the leader recognizes that adding new ideas and new approaches to teaching may create chaotic patterns for some people. As people work to integrate new information into patterns, it may result in unhappiness or conflict. This is to be expected. The leader does not respond in anger or confrontation but recognizes the need to continue to develop meaningful patterns for the faculty.

The Brain Is Reflective

Chris Argyris and Donald Schön (1996) describe what they term "double loop learning." This is learning that challenges the patterns in our current thinking. Single loop learning is consistent with our current beliefs and thinking and is easily integrated and learned. Double loop learning, however, requires a fundamental change in our thinking. In order to accomplish this fundamental change, we use the reflective part of our brain. The brain must literally reconstruct its knowledge. Reflection is the process by which existing knowledge is reframed and refined into new knowledge. Thus, the brain accesses current knowledge to evaluate the possibilities inherent in new information. This is a multifaceted activity as the brain considers all the possibilities of incorporation. This reflection not only is precipitated by major challenges to existing patterns but also can occur from the most mundane life activities. The brain is consciously and unconsciously rearranging information, evaluating multiple responses, and making new patterns of meaning. This reflective process is invaluable to the courageous leader. By activating the reflective processes of the brain, the leader can evaluate actions and reconsider strategies to achieve the school's vision. Knowing the importance of this activity, the leader can model reflection and encourage the faculty and staff to engage in daily reflection on the teaching-learning process. New knowledge that is a part of the culture of the school can be created.

The Human Brain Is Remarkable

The brain has a high degree of plasticity that allows it to change in response to experience. People learn and change throughout their lifetimes. Social interactions are essential to developing the neural networks required for the development of language and thinking. Emotions are the neural responses that allow the brain to respond in ways that increase the likelihood of survival. As new information is experienced, the brain seeks to incorporate that knowledge into complex patterns. The more rich the environment, the more complex the patterns constructed. It is through the process of reflection that the brain is able to take apart old information and rearrange it into new and more meaningful information. The processes of reconstructing knowledge are facilitated when the new information provides the structures of planning and organization that serve as templates of innovation.

COURAGEOUS LEADERSHIP

Accepting the role and responsibilities of leadership leads to a road filled with obstacles and opportunities. Courage is a trait found in all great leaders. It will take courage to change the culture of a school from twentieth-century thinking to following brain-based learning principles in the classroom. But courage is not a trait that is only given to some. Anyone can develop courage. Courage is the quality of standing by one's beliefs and having the strength of conviction to do the right thing for children.

Courage begins with overcoming one's fears and insecurities. It is the willingness to take the calculated risk. And it is this willingness to take the risk that will inspire others on the campus. While all leaders need the basic skills to lead a group, this is not enough. The skills that are taught in traditional leadership courses, communication, decision making, and conflict resolution lay the foundation for good leadership. However, it is the inner drive to "take a stand" that develops the trust and admiration of others. Courage consists of trying new approaches, developing confidence in others, and speaking to the difficult issues that arise. Courage is not a new idea. Aristotle named courage as the first virtue because it is the virtue that makes all other virtues possible. Without the courage to act, trust, and speak, a leader is at best a caretaker of the present and at worst the harbinger of doom for the school.

The Courage Principles

Being a courageous leader requires understanding the change process and applying brain-based principals while being a person of integrity.

C   Communicate in Ways Consistent with Brain-Based Principles

Communicate with images that evoke emotions while also providing frequent repetition of the purposes and vision of your school. This establishes the neural networks and memory to establish new patterns in the brain. It creates a sense of confidence in times of change and innovation. Although the future is unknowable, help the faculty envision this future through stories of past experiences, a sharing of the current reality, and a path that clearly leads to a new future.

O   Operate with Integrity

As the leader of the school, one must provide complete honesty in everything done or said. Beliefs about people, the school, and learning must align with one's actions. Even when one makes a mistake, one must truthfully admit that mistake and work toward correcting it. As a leader, every action reflects one's character whether in the office, a classroom, a parent meeting, or a local restaurant. The faculty is observing the leader and forming beliefs about that individual. Those who are followers seek order and relationship. If information is not consistent with the established patterns of belief about the school leader, new patterns that incorporate this inconsistency will form. Living up to one's word allows the faculty to develop trust in the leader and establishes a culture (pattern) of ethical behavior.

U   Understand the Change Process

The change process is messy and will not happen easily. Realize that the brain takes time to assimilate new knowledge into meaningful patterns. Provide the structures of dialogue, decision making, and planning that facilitate the process. Learn how change happens and how change affects both knowledge and emotions. Use this knowledge of the change process to influence the faculty's emotions in ways that lead to progress and fulfillment of the school's vision.

R   Reflect as a Part of Practice

The brain can challenge its own thinking as well as the thinking of others. Cultivate a culture of reflection. Through the process of reflection, your faculty finds patterns and looks for meaning. Reflection allows the faculty to learn from experiences.

A   *Apply Brain-Based Principles*

Recognize the need for people to interact, have time to reflect, and make meaning of new ideas and experiences. Immerse the faculty in the process of developing new ideas and strategies that facilitate learning. Provide ample time for both individual and group reflection.

G   *Grow in Your Leadership*

Just as leaders need to provide new information to the faculty and teams, they must also continue to read and reflect about leadership and brain-based learning. Lifelong learning is not just a phrase to a courageous leader.

E   *Evaluate the Process*

Evaluation is essential to leading with courage. Evaluation is an ongoing habit that builds on the reflective process and provides the information necessary to rethink and revise.

Leadership of today's schools is challenging and risky. Taking risks implies the possibility of failure, and that can be frightening. Fear is overcome through courage. But courage is essential to building confidence in one's ability to lead. Patterns of courage are already present in every leader's brain. Each time a leader has faced a fearful situation and successfully navigated through that situation, a pattern for courage and confidence is established. This pattern of courage is enhanced by knowledge about change, knowledge about how the brain works, and a character with integrity.

Reflection is essential to the courageous leader's success. It is not the answers one finds that are most important but the questions one asks during times of reflection. The questions point the way to what is right for the school to achieve excellence in ways that are consistent with how the brain learns. The courage to lead a school to new levels of excellence based on brain-based learning principles is a unique opportunity that touches the leader's spirit at a basic level. Fear no longer influences decisions, but rather the leader makes decisions based on what is right for the children and right for the school. An open and honest approach to others engenders a culture of cooperation and collaboration that allows the social brain to build new patterns for achieving excellence. Leading with courage is not easy, but it is the right way to lead.

REFERENCES

Argyris, C., & Schön, D. (1996). *Organizational learning II: Theory, method and practice*. Reading, MA: Addison Wesley.

Bateson, G. (1970, January 9). Form, substance, and difference. Nineteenth Annual Korzybski Memorial Lecture. Institute of General Semantics, Forest Hills, NY.

Bridges, W. (2009). *Managing transitions*. Boston: Nicholas Brealey Publishing.

Capra, F. (1982). *The turning point: Science, society, and the rising culture*. New York: Simon & Schuster.

Dickman, M., & Blair, N. (2002). *Connecting leadership to the brain*. Thousand Oaks, CA: Corwin.

Green, R. (2013). *Practicing the art of leadership: A problem-based approach to implementing the ISLLC standards*. Boston: Pearson.

Greenleaf, R. (2002). *Servant leadership: A journey into the nature of legitimate power and greatness*. Mahwah, NJ: Paulist Press.

Kotter, J. (2012). *Leading change*. Boston: Harvard Business School Press.

Kouzes, J., & Posner, B. (2007). *The leadership challenge* (4th ed.). San Francisco: Jossey-Bass.

Kubler-Ross, E. (1997). *On death and dying*. New York: Scribner.

Lewin, K. (1947). *Frontiers in group dynamics*. Indianapolis: Bobbs-Merrill.

Logue, C. (1969). Come to the edge. In *New numbers* (pp. 65–66). London: Cape.

Ridley, M. (1996). *The origins of virtue: Human instincts and the evolution of cooperation*. New York: Penguin.

Rock, D., & Page, L. (2009). Coaching with the brain in mind: Foundations for practice. Hoboken, NJ: Wiley.

Russell, B. (1956). Mathematical logic as based on the theory of types. In R. S. March (Ed.), *Bertrand Russell: Logic and knowledge; Essays 1901–1950*. London: George.

Schwartz, J. (2002). *The mind and the brain*. New York: HarperCollins.

Senge, P. (2006). *The fifth discipline: The art and practice of the learning organization*. New York: Doubleday.

Siegel, D. (2012). *The developing mind: How relationships and the brain interact to shape who we are* (2nd ed.). New York: Guilford.

Whitehead, A. N., & Russell, B. (1910). *Principia mathematica.* Cambridge: Cambridge University Press.

Chapter Ten

Coda

There You Have It!

Timothy B. Jones

The starting point of all achievement is desire. Keep this constantly in mind. Weak desires bring weak results, just as a small amount of fire makes a small amount of heat! Desire is the starting point of all achievement, not a hope, not a wish, but a keen pulsating desire, which transcends everything. When your desires are strong enough you will appear to possess superhuman powers to achieve.

—Napoleon Hill

There you have it . . . the science, the proof, and the plan. The question becomes, "Do you have the desire to make a difference?" Despite a slow start, the good news is that more and more teachers and educational leaders are making the effort to create brain-compatible schools because, simply, it is the right thing to do for learners. Human beings are natural learners—if educators will just let them learn naturally. It is imperative that schools do just that, especially given all the stimuli (Internet, video games, and cell phones) that educators must compete with for the attention of learners. We know what to do—the research and technology are readily available—we just need to get on with doing it.

This final chapter is devoted to the voices, insights, and thoughts of school leaders and teachers who have taken this journey over the past year or more, and a few parting thoughts of encouragement are included. These are courageous educators that were not part of the case studies in chapters 5 and 6 but who wanted to offer their insights and encouragement to anyone who has the desire to use this incredible knowledge for making learning better, easier, and more fun for students. They come from numerous schools including high-performing, low-performing, and everything in between. This is one of the things that make brain-compatible learning implementation so important—it is not just for low-performing schools. It is for any school that wants students performing at peak potential. It is for all learners, because it is natural for all learners, including adults!

VOICES FROM THE FIELD

One courageous leader, Tami Nauyokas at Cooper Junior High School, who along with a team of middle school principals in her district, decided to implement brain-compatible math in all seventh- and eighth-grade math classes, recalls,

> Students who have fun learning cannot help but learn and remember more. It became very apparent that students enjoyed doing high-level thinking activities more than the traditional skill-drills practice they had done in the past. Profound learning was definitely taking place in our math classes, and we have similar expectations for science this year. (Jones, 2012, p. 18)

Brain-compatible math teacher Jennifer Hart at McMillan Junior High, who was part of the same math initiative, speaks from experience when she proclaimed,

> The brain is so complex and multifaceted. The more understanding teachers have of the adolescent brain and its functions, especially the frontal lobe, the better understanding teachers have of how their students learn and process information. Any activity, assignment, or worksheet can be revised and implemented so that a teacher can become a facilitator of learning and not just a lecturer. The key to success is to start small and build a repertoire of lessons that are engaging and successful for all students. All students can learn through brain-based lessons. The students should be the ones tired at the end of the day and not the teachers!

Not so surprising, students like brain-compatible learning, too. Although it takes a little time for students to become accustomed to being responsible for their own learning (remember they learned the traditional way for many years), once they are acclimated they immediately see the benefits and success of their engagement. Principal Jon Peters, also at

Textbox 10.1. An algebra teacher's classroom story
One of my favorite brain-based algebra stories comes from a class that did not start out well. I was given a group of twelve sophomore and junior students who had failed algebra the prior year(s). Those in charge decided that the students would be double-blocked into my classroom for two periods right before lunch. Anxious to get to work with these kids, I was ready for the challenge, or so I thought. What I soon found was that they had failed due to not a lack of foundational knowledge but missing effort, absences, and some behavior problems. They did not want anything to do with math and made that clear by refusing to work from the first day, yet they would be in my classroom for two periods a day, all year. It was a very long first semester while I strived to make the math interesting and relevant to their lives, to develop their understanding and critical-thinking skills, and then place them in a position where it was less painful to work hard in class than to goof off and waste time. There were small victories, but some days the only thing I helped to develop was a bad headache. Their success appeared elusive.

BRAIN-COMPATIBLE LEARNING TO THE RESCUE!

Second semester rolled around, and we then had the full support of our brain-based consultants who had already brought the administration up to speed on the benefits of altering instruction to meet the needs of the students' long-term memories. The accomplishments that followed for that Algebra I class were astonishing. Although there were four teams, for the sake of simplicity I will focus on one team of three students. In hope that the vice principal would continue to support and promote the brain-based methods that woke up even our most reluctant students, he was invited to see the class in action. He said that he might stop by for a few minutes during the first half of class. I announced to the class that we may have a visitor and asked them to please just continue as if there was no one else in the room. Jocelyn, not unfamiliar with being called to the office, expressed concern. "We better not argue then, right? We'll be good." Typically, she and Laney would argue with each other and with another student, Dro, over the math as they worked through the activities and follow-up practice problems. I ensured them that not only were such disputes okay but also the vice-principal would be very happy to hear them debate the math. Their mouths dropped open, and they started to laugh as they exclaimed, "So, we are supposed to argue about the math?" What took place next was a joy. The activity was designed to lead the students down a path to discover the solution to a system of equations.

For forty-five minutes, these three students bantered back and forth, often quite loudly and always with enthusiasm, as they worked through the activity. The three of them started with just as many solutions, narrowed it to two, and finally down to one solution, but reached through three different methods: Laney used a table; Jocelyn, a graph; and Dro's preference was "common sense" as he made use of the patterns he recognized. After all three agreed, they went from team to team arguing their point. Once all teams settled on the same conclusion, they were given a few practice problems similar to the activity, and finally they spent the last thirty minutes solving systems of equations using various methods they had basically taught themselves.

The vice principal, who slipped in just before the bell and planned to watch for about fifteen minutes, stayed the full length of the double-blocked period. Yes, students, teachers, and administrators truly enjoy the learning that is brain compatible. These students could learn the math well; they just needed to be guided to learn in a way that stimulated cognitive conflict and then afforded them the time and patience to reach resolution!

—Julie Haba, Algebra I teacher
Nimitz High School
Irving Independent School District

McMillan Junior High School, offered this student testimonial from his campus: "I love this brain stuff! My head hurts when the class is over, but it is great when we get to do it" (Jones, 2012, p. 17). Justin Terry of Burnett Junior High School and another principal in the same district added,

On our campus, students continually stated that they had never learned math this way before and it was actually fun. The students struggled at first, creating the cognitive conflict needed to make the learning connection. However, once the connection was made, the looks on their faces were priceless. Brain/mind instruction has transformed the traditional repetition and process-based mathematics in our math instruction into meaningful and application-based, long-term learning opportunities. Learning is truly centered on learners! (Jones, 2012, p. 17)

Creativity is critical in a brain-enriched environment as students truly become the center of learning and constructors of their own knowledge. Student teacher Greg Potter, who studied under Hart, adds, "Self-discovery led to every advancement made throughout mankind. Brain-based lessons introduce students to discovery. Teachers witness many 'a-ha' moments when offering student-driven discovery prior to the official introduction of a concept." Julie Haba, a teacher at Nimitz High School, further offers,

> Brain-based learning energized our Algebra I classroom! If that had been the only result, I would have been a big fan. Bonus: with that energy came active students, eagerly talking about the math with each other. They were interested in sharing ideas, working through the challenges in many different ways, and then joining forces to compare their methods and solutions with the other teams, all while enjoying every minute of it. Most importantly, in May they could even recall and apply knowledge from the beginning of the year. As anyone who has ever had teenagers in their classroom knows, this sounds like heaven. The exciting news is, it is *not* too good to be true and requires only trust in the process and patience.

Teachers, administrators, and students believe in the merits of natural and brain-compatible learning. What about other school stakeholders? Nauyokas continues her insights:

> The buzz among students about something in math being fun quickly spread around the district. Students were excited and talking about their math work outside of their math classes and outside of school. Central administration and the school board took note and became very supportive when they were able to hear students and teachers both express how much fun and success they were having in class with the brain/mind learning activities.

Nauyokas and the group of middle schools implementing brain-compatible math produced a video for presentation at a school board meeting, and on YouTube, to keep the board and community in the loop about their implementation.

Pine Tree Independent School District superintendent T. J. Farler adds,

> Students, teachers, and administrators must all experience cognitive dissonance in order to learn and grow in our work. Instruction that is designed and centered on the learner is critical for deep learning and learning that is retained over time. The design and the intent of brain-based instruction do

exactly that—it engages the learner and ensures that the learning is meaningful and retained over time. (Jones, 2011, p. 18)

Farler believes in a hands-on approach by every administrator in her district, and thus cautions,

It is essential that the campus principal leads, participates, and experiences brain-based instruction with the teachers. The principal must lead the effort, monitor the work (teachers and students) in the classroom, and collaborate with the teachers during the professional learning process. Otherwise, it's just another one-time workshop with no lasting change in teacher behavior. (Jones, 2011, p. 18)

Haba, also thinking about other stakeholders, reflects that "skeptical teachers and administrators become believers when those standardized test scores come back!" When asked what advice she has for teachers contemplating this change to instruction, she gleams,

Jump in with both feet and consistently use this instructional method to the best of your ability; don't worry about being "perfect." Teachers will get better and better at execution as time goes on, but a half-hearted attempt will not produce the amazing results we work so hard to achieve for each of our students.

Allowing as much time as is needed for the students to struggle to figure things out is the most critical component, and we can all exercise patience. Use only questions, no answers, to guide the students in the direction you know they need to go during the activities and follow-up. Finally, have fun! Brain-based learning is like a room full of fresh air in the springtime. It is my firm belief that *all* students want to learn well; they simply need to have the faith that they can and the freedom to do it.

It takes a big commitment on the part of teachers and administrators to bring such systemic change. Even so, it is clear that the fruit to bear makes the commitment and hard work well worth it for the school and ultimately the students. Schools need more excitement, and that excitement must start with the adults in the school (Jones, 2012). Schools can never be exciting for students if they are not exciting for the adults who are navigating the educational enterprise. When the brain is excited, it is naturally motivated, and that intrinsic motivation results in more brain resources being dedicated to the task at hand.

SOME THOUGHTS GOING FORWARD

This final chapter opened with a quote by Napoleon Hill stressing how important desire is in achievement. A professional can have the knowledge and the capacity to do something, but without the desire to do it, without a deep, real desire that gives birth to commitment, the knowledge and capacity are useless. The truth is that many professional educators have the knowledge and capacity to make an enormous impact on children or learning, yet they spend most if not all of their time maintaining the status quo. The public education system has an immense intrinsic resistance to change as discussed in chapter 1. Over time, that resistance has contributed to the loss of confidence in the system itself and continues to contribute to the loss of public school market share.

The exciting news is that like-minded and committed professional educators of every level are working hard to change the trend. The innovation and advanced pedagogical practices that have been presented in this book are paving a better and more natural way for students to learn. While the United States may be behind some other countries in using this groundbreaking innovation, we also have the capacity to catch up and move ahead once again. The question that remains seems to be, "Do we have the desire?" Desire allows us to use the knowledge, find the courage, and take the risk in order to make a difference. Desire is the first step . . . the only first step. Desire leads to commitment. Without the desire there is no second step. In fact, without the desire, the status quo can only be the result.

International motivational speaker Paul Vitale (1998), who just happens to be a dear friend and fraternity brother, says, "You can't finish unless you begin" (p. 9). Educators have obviously begun something professionally (so there is some desire for something), so the obvious question is, "What are they trying to finish?" Is the desire the status quo? Is the desire for the continued loss of public school market share? Is the desire simply the path of least resistance? For the contributors of this book, the common denominator is clearly a better school for children that stops the erosion of confidence in the very system in which they work. They have found their way to reject the status quo and move toward something different and better. Somehow we overcame the resistance of the system in order to move and lead the system in this new and innovative way.

So we ask our reader, Based on what is likely to be your result, what seems to be your desire? As an educator, what will your epitaph or your legacy be when you finish? "What do you desire it to be?" "How does your professional practice support that desire?" As Geoffrey Caine suggests in the foreword, our hope is that this book bridges theory with practice, knowledge with action. Our desire was to take everything we collectively understand about learning and leading and help other educators apply it to their practice and to their schools or school districts. Our work over the past twenty years has been exciting for us and for the students ultimately impacted by our efforts. How or even will you use what we learned to impact yours? Regardless of your journey and whichever role you decide is yours to play, we admire your desire to make a difference and wish you Godspeed!

REFERENCES

Jones, T. B. (2012). How exciting are schools for adults? *Insight: Journal of the Texas Association of School Administrators, 27*(4), 18–19.

Jones, T. B. (2011). Schools find brain research key to student engagement and improving performance in math. *Insight: Journal of the Texas Association of School Administrators, 26*(3), 17–18.

Vitale, P. (1998). *Are you puzzled by the puzzle of life? Lessons to remember as you pursue your purpose.* Little Rock, AR: Walsworth.

Editor/Author
and Contributor Biographies

ABOUT THE EDITOR/AUTHOR

Timothy B. Jones, EdD, is associate professor of educational leadership and policy at Sam Houston State University and the principal consultant for the consulting firm that bears his name. He holds a bachelor of arts in political science and general business from Stephen F. Austin State University (SFASU) and a master of science from the University of Houston at Clear Lake in educational management. In 2000, he completed his doctor of education in educational leadership, also from SFASU.

Since 1984, Jones has spent his career in school improvement in the roles of teacher, administrator, and now professor and consultant. While at the University of Texas at Tyler, he cofounded the Principal and Superintendent Institute, which worked with hundreds of school leaders in school-improvement initiatives by partnering with Geoffrey Caine of the Caine Learning Center. His inspiration for the institute grew from the School-within-a-School he began at Thomas J. Rusk Middle School in the Nacogdoches Independent School District. The program, "The Silver Team," utilized brain-enriched learning that concentrated on individualized and self-paced instruction for middle school students across the curriculum. The program was the focus of one installment of *Promising Practices in Texas Education*, produced by KLRN, the PBS station in San Antonio.

In order to return to his first love—teaching—Jones left his administrative practice in 1998 to begin his professoriate career. Since that time, he has authored more than seventy publications and made over 130 presentations, keynotes, and in-services. He is a past president of both the

Texas Council of Professors of Educational Administration (TCPEA) and the SFASU chapter of Phi Delta Kappa. He is currently the editor of the highly regarded *School Leadership Review*. The Texas Congress of Parents and Teachers bestowed an Honorary Life Membership upon him in 1990, and the Texas House of Representatives flew a Texas flag over the capitol for him "In Recognition of His Dedication and Impact to the Education Community of Texas" on May 29, 2009. Jones makes his home in Dallas, Texas. For more information, see http://www.timothybjones.net/.

ABOUT THE CONTRIBUTORS

Geoffrey Caine, LLM, is executive director of Caine Learning LLC. He is a learning consultant, writer, and process coach, and he works throughout the United States and overseas. Geoffrey and his wife were recently international colleagues for Learning to Learn, a ten-year leading-edge reform effort involving more than two hundred schools in South Australia. He has coauthored nine books and many chapters and articles on learning and education, including *Strengthening and Enriching Your Professional Learning Community: The Art of Learning Together* in 2010. A tenth book is under contract to Teachers' College Press. Caine has made presentations at many international, national, and regional conferences and meetings. These range from the American Society for Training and Development and the Association for Supervision and Curriculum Development to the Eighth International Conference on Thinking and the World Conference on Education for All. Geoffrey and his wife Renate reside in Idyllwild, California.

Renate N. Caine, PhD, is executive director of the Natural Learning Research Institute and professor emerita of education, California State University–San Bernardino. Caine consults throughout the world on natural learning. She has taught or worked with teachers at every level from kindergarten to the university level. Her work with schools has been featured on *Teacher TV* on the Discovery Channel, *Wizards of Wisdom* shown on PBS, and elsewhere. She has published extensively. Her first book, written with her husband, was *Making Connections: Teaching and the Human Brain*. Their most recent book is *Natural Learning for a Con-*

nected World: Education, Technology and the Human Brain, published in 2011. Joseph Chilton Pierce writes in the foreword, "And right here I stick my neck out and state unequivocally that *Natural Learning for a Connected World* towers over and is easily the most remarkable, intelligent, and challenging work I have read on the subject of learning, schooling, social crises and the like, and weighs heavily into the whole issue of development." Renate and her husband Geoffrey made their home in Idyllwild, California.

Peggy B. Gill, EdD, is professor of educational leadership in the Department of Educational Leadership and Policy Studies at the University of Texas at Tyler (UTT). She earned a doctorate in educational leadership from Stephen F. Austin State University, and prior to serving in the professoriate she was a classroom teacher, diagnostician, behavior consultant, and building administrator. She works with school districts in the area of change and most recently served as director of Tyler GEAR UP, a six-year federal grant to increase high school graduation and enrollment in college. She served as a faculty member for the Principal and Superintendent Institute at UTT. Gill currently lives in The Colony, Texas, a suburb of Dallas.

Beverly J. Irby, EdD, is Texas State University System Regents' Professor in the Department of Educational Leadership and Counseling at Sam Houston State University. Her research involves issues regarding social justice activism, such as curricular development and the administration of bilingual/ESL instruction, early childhood interventions, gifted education, and women's leadership issues. Irby resides in Huntsville, Texas.

Patrick M. Jenlink, EdD, is professor of doctoral studies in the Department of Secondary Education and Educational Leadership at Stephen F. Austin State University. He also serves as director of the Educational Research Center. He earned his doctorate in educational administration from Oklahoma State University, and prior to serving in the professoriate he was a classroom teacher, counselor, building administrator, and superintendent of schools. Jenlink inspires his students with the works of John Dewey, the Socratic method, change, and he models constructivism. Several of his former doctoral students are authors in this book and clearly reflect those beliefs. Patrick has authored dozens of articles and book chapters in addition to authoring six books. He is also the editor of *Teacher Education and Practice* and coeditor of *Scholar-Practitioner Quarterly*. He makes his home with his wife Karen in Nacogdoches, Texas.

Lawrence Kohn, PhD, is director for program and evaluation for the Rice Education Entrepreneurship Program (REEP) at Rice University. An educator of thirty-one years, he is a former principal, professor, and English teacher. He is a published author of multiple articles and book chapters. His research interests are in Professional Learning Community, assessment, leadership, and high school reform and redesign. He received his doctorate in curriculum and instruction from the University of Houston (2001), his master of education in historical, social, and cultural foundations from the University of Houston (1996), and his bachelor of science in English from Youngstown State University (1982). Kohn lives in Houston, Texas.

Rafael Lara-Alecio, PhD, is professor and director of bilingual education programs in the Department of Educational Psychology at Texas A&M University. His primary areas of research are in assessment, language development, evaluation, and bilingual content-area instruction. He is coauthor of a pedagogical theory and model for transitional English bilingual classrooms. Lara-Alecio lives in College Station, Texas.

Genie Bingham Linn, EdD, is an associate professor in the Department of Educational Leadership and Policy Studies at the University of Texas at Tyler. There she teaches in the graduation program for principal preparation by guiding students through their own action research projects. Before Linn earned her doctorate in educational administration from Stephen F. Austin State University, she was a high school English teacher, an educational consultant, and a high school principal. Her thirty years of Texas public school experiences inform her book chapter contributions to *Texas Public School Organization and Administration*. She shares her interest in leadership voice in journal publications, and through her work as editor for the *Journal of Texas Women School Executives*, she supports the voices of women leaders. Linn resides in Hideaway, Texas.

Camille Malone was director of mathematics for the Dallas Independent School District (DISD) for twelve years. She holds a bachelor's degree in mathematics from the University of North Texas, a master's degree in interdisciplinary studies with a concentration in philosophy and political economy from the University of Texas, and she has completed coursework toward a doctorate in educational administration at Texas A&M University–Commerce. Her doctoral work is concentrated in brain-based, experiential learning, particularly in mathematics. She has been a speaker at the National Conference on Educational Excellence and Economic Growth, and also a keynote at the Charlotte Mecklenburg Educational Conference. Malone is a recipient of the Jim Collins Outstanding Teacher Award and the Dallas Independent School District Teacher of the Year. In 2012, she retired from DISD after forty years and is now a full-time mathematics consultant and adjunct professor. She resides in Rockwall, Texas.

Linda Rodriguez, EdD, is area superintendent in Aldine Independent School District and adjunct in bilingual/ESL at Sam Houston State University. Her administrative career includes having served as principal of a Montessori bilingual prekindergarten campus, as area superintendent of urban prekindergarten through twelfth-grade schools, and as administrator supervising the early college campus.

Ross B. Sherman, EdD, earned his doctorate at the University of Houston and holds a master's and bachelor's degree from Temple University. He is a former elementary teacher, assistant principal, and principal. Currently he is serving as professor and chair of the Department of Educational Leadership and Policy Studies at the University of Texas at Tyler. Sherman's body of work in school improvement utilizing brain-compatible instruction culminated with his cofounding of the Principal and Superintendent Institute, also at UTT. He is a longtime resident of Tyler, Texas.

Fuhui Tong, PhD, is assistant professor in the Department of Educational Psychology at Texas A&M University. Her research focuses on program and teacher factors on English learners' school success and quantitative methodology in bilingual/ESL education. Tong has been involved in federal and state projects on reducing educational inequality for English learners. Tong calls College Station, Texas, home.